VIEWS FROM THE TOP

VIEWS FROM THE TOP

Establishing the Foundation for the Future of Business

Edited by
Jerome M. Rosow
President, Work in America Institute, Inc.

Facts On File Publications
New York, New York ● Oxford, England

Views From the Top

Copyright © 1985 by Jerome M. Rosow

Library of Congress Cataloging in Publication Data

Rosow, Jerome M.
    Views from the top.

    1. Industrial management—United States—Case studies.
2. Corporations—United States—Case studies. 3.Public
relations—United States—Case studies. I. Title.
HD70.U5R65 1985   658   84-10127
ISBN 0-8160-1123-0

Composition by Facts On File/Circle Graphics
Printed by Haddon Craftsmen

1   2   3   4   5   6   7   8   9   10

ACKNOWLEDGMENTS

Two of my associates made it possible for this book to become a reality rather than an unfulfilled dream. Carol Nardi, my executive assistant, directed the search for contributing authors. This involved a determined and sustained program of selling the idea and following through until the completed manuscript of each important, busy contributor was actually in her hands. She was never discouraged and didn't take no for an answer.

Beatrice Walfish, editorial director of Work in America Institute, exercised her talents as editor and organizer and assisted me with the Introduction and Summing Up chapter as well as coordinating all work with the publisher. She was indispensable.

Kate Kelly, my editor at Facts On File, proved to be one of those unique editors who makes a personal commitment to each book, and follows through to its completion. She gave unselfishly of her time and energy, her editorial skills and her enthusiasm throughout the life of this project.

To Rosalyn
—my wife, CEO and guiding spirit.

CONTENTS

INTRODUCTION

Views from the Top comprises the personal statements of nine business leaders from their unique perspective as chief executives of several of America's best-known corporations. In a special sense, the book is also my own personal statement on the role of leadership in corporate life, based on the insights and understandings acquired in 40 years as an active participant in private enterprise and public affairs.

As an executive in Exxon over a period of 24 years, I observed the high reaches of corporate life at first hand. As assistant secretary of labor from 1969 to 1971 and, after that, as founder and president of Work in America Institute, a nonprofit work research organization dedicated to the advancement of productivity and quality of working life, I was—and am—personally concerned with the effectiveness of work organizations in America and in the free world. In these several careers, I came to the inevitable conclusion that the performance of a large enterprise and its responsiveness to change depend to a large degree on the role played by the chief executive officer, the CEO.

No corporation, no CEO, performs in a vacuum; both are subject to the sociological, economical and technological changes in the society in which they operate. These changes have been both rapid and far-reaching during the last 20 years. Changing values and attitudes, increased education, the explosive growth of the work force, the high-tech information age and the volatile world economy have combined to create a climate of instability. Other unsettling factors have been the demand for participation in decision making on the job, the continuing need for new skills, the insecurity of employment, the constant pressure for profitability and the intensification of world competition.

Additional pressures have been imposed by financial raiders, deregulation of entire industries, mergers and takeovers, leveraged buyouts, corporate failures and divestitures, including major bankruptcies. Little wonder that the stable organizations of the 1960s have largely given way in the 1980s to dynamic enterprises that must fight for their survival, and that the continuity of even the largest corporations is no longer assured.

Increased pressures on the corporation—from whatever source—have conferred both enormous power and, at the same time, great responsibility on the individual CEO. The CEO succeeds or fails—or muddles through—to the extent that he has a grasp of the emerging needs of the society and the economy. Increasingly, his responsiveness to the outside world determines his ability to judge the future correctly, take risks and lead the corporation. At the same time, he must look inward and remain in close touch with the organization and the people who are critical to performance and corporate potential.

While the instability of corporate life in recent years has contributed little to the CEO's peace of mind, it has increased the newsworthiness of the corporation. The rise and fall of companies and their leaders now dominate the front pages rather than the business sections of the nation's newspapers—and the evening news on television is as likely to feature the problems of a major company as the details of a national or international crisis.

With the emergence of the corporation as a dominant force, Americans are increasingly curious about the inner workings of big business. Best sellers with business themes abound, but most of them have been written by third parties at least once removed from the real world. Academics and creative analysts have drawn some interesting conclusions, but they have based them on management practices known to them only through study and observation or, possibly, research. These volumes are more than an arm's length away from the actual organization, and are usually prepared independent of the perceptions, ideas and personal values of the incumbent CEOs.

This high level of public interest in the actual workings of corporate America reflects much more than simple curiosity.

It underlines the public perception of the power and influence of multibillion dollar, multinational corporations on all facets of American life and on individual Americans.

Views from the Top seeks to respond to the deep interest of the public in the inside story of corporations by presenting the viewpoints of nine major corporate leaders, drawn from various sectors of the economy. Their chapters differ from the current rash of best sellers in that they are firsthand accounts of the inner workings of corporations by the people who are most responsible for their well-being. And they are written in their own way.

The chief executives who contributed to *Views* were invited to do so in a format that they felt was appropriate. The freedom to speak their own minds on whatever aspect of the company or of their tenure they chose resulted in nine remarkable chapters from nine men who represent, in many ways, a cross-section of America's business leaders. Each of them undertook the assignment because he had a particular interest in sharing his personal style of corporate leadership with the general public. Each of them made a commitment to expend considerable time and effort in setting forth his views.

The reader observes at close range how these chief executives visualize their role in the corporation—their participation in strategic decision making, buying and selling entire businesses, realigning their organizations, managing growth, changing corporate cultures—and how this role is used in evaluating and planning for the future. Their accounts are revealing not only in what they choose to discuss but in what they omit.

They are not concerned here with their climb to success or their personal triumphs—nor do they refer to personal style or to personality as distinct from substance. Shareholder relations and the perceptions of the financial community are rarely mentioned. The authors are not preoccupied with government and politics, nor are they addicted to the jargon, slogans or buzz words endemic in prevailing management literature. The authors get to the heart of the matter with direct, plain-talking accounts of what seems important to them as the CEOs of leading corporations. They address the present always in terms of the future. And they view the corporation and its functions in relation to the changing needs of customers, current and potential. By joining together in this single volume, they have created a work in which the sum is far greater than its parts.

Henry Wendt (SmithKline Beckman) articulates his views on the future of the American corporation—specifically on how the corporation should be reorganized to respond to the vast demographic, social and economic changes in the world. He proposes a new model of the American corporation based on a broad and far-reaching set of values and goals and sees the CEO as "the nucleus of the living organism of the corporation" and as "the regulator of its metabolism."

Robert Anderson (Rockwell International) is the ideal spokesman for diversification in American industry. Directing a high-tech, multi-industry corporation, with $9 million in sales, he defines the role of the CEO in managing four distinct businesses in a broad variety of markets. He discusses the unique balancing act whereby diversity spreads the risk and helps the corporation maintain steady growth through present and future peaks and valleys in the business cycle.

Charles L. Brown (AT&T) reveals how he directed the virtual break-up of the largest corporation in the world. The traumatic shocks inflicted upon the corporation by government action required a radical reshaping of the nation's telecommunications structure and the creation of a new corporate structure that was modern, flexible and strong enough to enter a new era of world competition.

Edward R. Telling (Sears, Roebuck) relates his classic achievements in redirecting the latent energies and talents of Sears into a model of growth and response to change. Adding the financial services of consumer banking, real estate and personal investments to the existing core of retailing was a brilliant form of diversification. Completed without upsetting the corporate culture or losing touch with the company's inherent strengths, this diversification has instead opened new profit centers for a forward-moving consumer-oriented giant.

Douglas Danforth (Westinghouse) relates how the corporate management committee manages this giant business, functioning as 26 separate and largely autonomous business units and operating with a high degree of independence. He describes the linkage among finance, technology and marketing functions and their relationship to one broad strategy tied to quality, productivity, portfolio direction, executive development and communications.

George Weissman (Philip Morris) traces the growth of Philip Morris as a corporation that succeeded as a David among Goliaths and that has never become complacent. This driving force fuels the culture and encourages managers to remain competitive.

William McGowan (MCI Communications) surprises the reader by omitting any references to the aggressive entry of MCI into the telecommunications industry. Instead, he shares his vision of the future in an era brought into being by the emergence of new computer, telecommunications and information technologies. He sees the information age as the greatest competitive challenge to date and explains why.

T. Mitchell Ford (Emhart Corporation) defines the importance of credibility in all corporate affairs as the sine quo non of successful leadership today and, in his estimation, in the future. He considers the role of the CEO a combination of counselor, arbitrator, philosopher and worrier.

Paul F. Oreffice (Dow Chemical) takes great pride in his unofficial title as the "phantom personnel director." He presents an insightful account of the inner workings of executive development, delegation and decision making at Dow.

Summing Up

These nine distinctive views provide a feast of ideas and insights. It is not unexpected to discover that many of these men share similar ideas, yet each chapter is different in emphasis and in the degree of attention devoted to a particular area.

I was pleased to find that a number of themes of major importance were represented. These themes were not assigned—or even suggested—when I invited the authors to contribute to this volume, and yet they have emerged as the special concerns of many of the contributors. Nine major themes predominate, to be discussed in greater detail in chapter 10.

Henry Wendt

Henry Wendt, president and chief executive officer of SmithKline Beckman Corporation, joined the company in 1955. He served in a variety of executive marketing positions in the United States and abroad before his election as president in April 1976 and his election as chief executive officer in February 1982. He is a member of the coporation's board of directors.

Mr. Wendt joined the corporation shortly after receiving his bachelor of arts degree in American diplomatic history in 1955 from Princeton University. His interest in international affairs led him to a career in international business, and he joined Smith Kline & French Laboratories, as it was known then, in the International Division. He has since been identified, personally and professionally, as an internationalist.

Mr. Wendt was first responsible for small markets in then obscure parts of the world in Latin America, the Near East and Africa. He subsequently was the company's representative in Hawaii, transferring to Montreal, Canada, in 1958, where he remained until 1961.

In 1962, he was responsible for the company's business in East Asia, a territory covering Japan through Southeast Asia, including the Philippine Islands. He established the company's first business in Japan with the introduction of SmithKline's cold medicine Contac.

Returning to Philadelphia in 1968, he was named vice-president and general manager, U.S. Pharmaceutical Products, in 1971. In 1973, he was appointed president,

Consumer Products, and a group vice-president in 1973. He was elected executive vice-president in 1974.

1
THE CORPORATION OF THE FUTURE

By Henry Wendt
President and Chief Executive Officer
SmithKline Beckman Corporation

In a historical context, the contemporary late twentieth century mulitinational corporation is a relatively new phenomenon. For all practical purposes, it is a phenomenon of post World War II. A few of today's large multinationals, although not known as such, existed before World War II. They tended to be very much the creatures of one individual, for example National Cash Register, IBM and Standard Oil.

But the professionally managed, publicly owned, large corporations with a global charter, organized to exist in perpetuity, are quite new. Consequently, the work of conceptualizing the purpose, structure and enduring value of these organizations continues to evolve. The concepts first used to describe corporate behavior in the 1940s and 1950s are for the most part out of date. The pace of corporate evolution continues; indeed, it has become more rapid and will probably continue to accelerate.

So, from the historical viewpoint, we are discussing an economic, political and social force that is still in the early stages of formation and has new and perhaps unimaginable forms and transmutations ahead of it. It is worth examining that entity now, however, to consider what its most appropriate model will be in the future.

THE EVOLUTION OF THE CORPORATE MODEL

While the corporate model advances at different paces in various countries, it is certainly possible to observe today the essential similarities in all the developed nations—Britain, Germany, France, Japan, the United States. Consequently, the companies used for illustrative purposes in this discussion are drawn from those nations. The current fad for Japanese management notwithstanding, there are lessons to be learned from the corporations of Japan as there are from a study of great American and European corporations. Where a national example is used, then, it is introduced to display the universal elements that apply everywhere. An objective discussion requires that we step above the battle of national management styles.

An important step in understanding the corporation and its structure was Peter Drucker's *The Concept of the Corporation*,[1] which appeared first in 1946 and has been reprinted several times.

In this book, Drucker examined the strategies of General Motors as it grew from a small company to a large industrial complex. The company was headed by Alfred P. Sloan, who continues to be viewed as the principal architect of the modern corporation. General Motors' methods of organization, management and finance were considered exemplary: a pyramidal structure, with an authority-driven, geometric approach, in which every problem must have a solution—a characteristic of nineteenth-century and early twentieth-century thought. I suppose one might call it the Euclidian concept of enterprise.

In the GM model, a number of divisions made and sold similar products, and General Motors used corporate staff techniques to achieve enormous efficiencies of scale by applying standard engineering approaches to its various automobile-making divisions.

It was a successful model for its time. And it was a natural step to the conglomerate, which resulted when the General Motors model of 1946 was carried to an exaggerated point. The conglomerate resulted when other corporations examined the divisionalized model and decided it worked so well that similar principles could be applied if multiple divisions were added to their existing corporate structures, often through acquisition, even though these divisions manufactured different products or supplied unrelated services. The common thread was supplied by strict planning and financial disciplines, many times from the desk of a strong authoritarian leader as in the case of Harold Geneen and ITT. But the technique did not work in most cases and frequently turned out to be a road to disaster. For example, we are currently treated to news reports that ITT is "refocusing" on its core business, electronic communications, amid speculation that ITT is now considered a "takeover" candidate.

The large multinational corporation, then, is in a state of evolution. As with other evolutionary phenomena, early stages of change in corporate adaptation are often only dimly perceived. The first mutants are obscured by old forms that have functioned effectively for generations.

The model for the contemporary corporation is largely based on nineteenth-century concepts of organization. Analogies to military prototypes are common. We still speak of staff and line functions and tend to view the organization as mechanical (rather than organic) with clearly discernible parts, each having a specialized function that contributes to the whole, but each a separate entity often not well integrated within the whole and in fact occasionally working at cross purposes with other parts of the organization.

In his tour de force, *A History of the World*,[2] Hugh Thomas details the life history of Vickers as an example of how nineteenth-century companies started, grew, diversified, lost momentum and in some cases were then subsidized by government, especially in the United Kingdom.

Vickers started out as a Sheffield steel manufacturer and a joint stock company in the 1860s, making steel for a wide variety of uses, including armaments. In 1897, Vickers acquired the Mavral Construction and Armaments Company at Barrow and a machine gun company. In 1902, Vickers bought Robert Napier's shipbuilding firm, which had built the early ironclads. In the same year, the company also bought a share of another shipbuilding firm at Glasgow.

After World War I, Vickers absorbed Armstrong-Whitworth,

which had been founded by William Armstrong in the first half of the nineteenth century with the then innovative use of hydraulic blast furnaces. Armstrong later produced armaments, founded an engineering firm, conceived the idea of using solar energy, began to make ships in 1868 and, in the 1890s, acquired Sir Joseph Whitworth's gun-making firm.

The enlarged and diversified Vickers survived (with government subsidies as early as 1924), but changed its organizational structure over the years as it attempted to adapt to Britain's changed role in world affairs.

Thomas observes: "This history of what became of one of Britain's largest firms is fairly characteristic of modern enterprise generally: an inspired founder, mergers, growth—and, in the end, a government subsidy when the firm has become so big as to be of national importance."

He notes that it is characteristic of large companies to become much more strictly disciplined as they increase in size and to be modeled, as I have noted, on structures similar to those of the nineteenth-century military forces.[3]

This description of the historical trajectory of corporations does not necessarily fit some leading U.S. companies; the authors of *In Search of Excellence* have drawn attention to important exceptions.[4] But for the most part, it fairly describes a great many, if not most, of the organizational patterns of the *Fortune* 200 companies. The national subsidization phenomenon, which has become a standard British cure for its ailing basic industries, has only recently been tried in the United States with the rescue of Lockheed, Chrysler and some U.S. banks. Of course, the pressure for voluntary restraint by Japan on exports of automobiles to the United States must also be considered an indirect form of subsidizing General Motors and the rest of the automobile industry.

REORGANIZATION—THE MODEL OF THE FUTURE

Multinational corporations have become the subject of intense scrutiny by members of academia and professional management consultants, who have suggested ways in which the corporation might reorganize to operate more effectively.

CEOs and managers are interested in these suggestions and in the experiences and insights of their peers. What form should the corporation take in response to demographic changes, altered expectations of populations and changing world markets?

The Conference Board recently conducted a study[5] of the views of 18 chief executives representing a broad range of well-regarded companies to explore their views on top-level staffing to manage strategic change. The Conference Board also surveyed more than 200 senior personnel executives to learn more about successful (and unsuccessful) executive-development approaches aimed at the same objective.

In the introduction to this report, the president of The Conference Board explained its rationale:

> A 1981 Conference Board survey found that, regardless of industry, the overwhelming majority of U.S. chief executives expected major changes in the character of their businesses and in their corporate strategies during the next three to five years. Moreover, again, regardless of industry, these CEOs ranked the development of the leadership for such strategic redirection as their most urgent top-management staffing challenge.[6]

As interesting as this study is, it focuses on the relatively short term. It suggests ways of developing strategic leadership in the '80s; but my interest runs beyond that. I am concerned with a new model of the corporation—the kind that will be in place, say, in the twenty-first century. And I am thinking of the future of large, publicly held corporations that would today be classified in the *Fortune* 200.

WORLD-ORIENTED ORGANIZATIONS

What is the role of these large corporations in our society? What is their purpose? Why should society tolerate these multibillion-dollar behemoths, with their massive concentrations of wealth and power? What can they contribute to the advancement of the planet? Peter Drucker has again tackled this question in a book in which he says that the power and wealth of large corporations impose responsibility.[7] But what is that responsibility?

The answer must surely go beyond the simplistic rationale that size yields economies of scale and efficiency, the traditional nineteenth-century response.

A more contemporary reply is that the purpose of multinational corporations is to pursue their science and technology, to create value from them, and then to bring their products and services to the world to enhance the quality of life and to improve human productivity.

If a corporation can make its science and technology applicable to only part of the world, it is not achieving full leverage or receiving the full return on its investment. We are compelled, therefore, to see the new model of the corporation as a wholly world-oriented organization. That is my first point about the future corporation, and it is fundamental.

ORGANIC VS. MECHANICAL ORGANIZATION

My second point is that if we agree that the large corporations I am speaking of have the purpose of serving society by improving the quality of life—in the case of SmithKline Beckman, through the pursuit of health care science and technology and the enhancement of the productivity of our customers—I believe it is essential that we operate as fully integrated organizations, where each of the parts supports some vital role of the other parts. In short, we must look at the corporations as organic, not mechanical.

This view is not exclusively my own; others have seen the merit of an organic organization. For example, Robert Eccles, assistant professor of business administration at Harvard University, contributed a stimulating analysis of the basic varieties of corporate organization to a recent Harvard Business School publication. He describes the organic organization as emphasizing "informality, networks of authority based on expertise rather than hierarchy, and high levels of stress and ambiguity."[8]

In organic organizations, he points out, responsibility exceeds authority, and he contrasts this with mechanical organizations based on military models, which have a clearly defined hierarchy of authority for decision making. Stress and ambiguity, he observes, are greatly reduced by the use of rules and procedures in mechanical organizations.

Perhaps I should add as an aside that stress and ambiguity are characteristic of life and reality, even of science, and even of such a precise discipline as mathematics. In 1931, Kurt Gödel showed with his Incompleteness Theorem that most logical propositions in mathematics are subject to ambiguity, thus modifying the certainty of many existing mathematical proofs. Similarly, in management we approach solutions to our problems, including organizational problems, with reason and logic; but the solutions are always only proximate, rarely absolute.

In an article in *Business Horizons*,[9] William Gordon, professor and coordinator of organizational studies at Kent State University, discusses the organic versus mechanical corporate models and makes the point that some structures better fit a given national culture than others. That is, national differences have implications for how a multinational is organized.

He illustrates the conflicting national values of some joint U.S.-Japan ventures, citing as failures Singer, Kraft Foods, TRW and Union Carbide, and notes that "the most crucial factor contributing to these failures is cultural managerial perspectives."[10]

While I agree that cultural considerations *modify* the structure of corporations, it seems to me that basic structural principles are transnational, as I have already noted, and that—certainly in the corporations of the long-term future—there will tend to be more similarities than differences in patterns of corporate organization throughout the world.

Gordon's view that "Americans do not want much power distance between superiors and subordinates" and his conclusion that in the United States a task-oriented and people-oriented management works best[11] are no doubt insights that are applicable to most evolving multinational corporations.

William Ouchi, in a book that has enjoyed a good deal of popularity in U.S. management circles,[12] suggests much the same solution for larger corporations: a return to a state of almost clam-like intimacy within operating units and more emphasis upon the organic concept of organization.

CONSOLIDATED VS. DIVERSIFIED ORGANIZATION

My third major point about the structure of the future model of the corporation is that by thinking of the corporation organically, we change our perspective on the nature of its organization, and we see many former management questions in a different light.

For example, an organic perspective necessarily rejects the concept of diversification through the acquisition or development of businesses unrelated to a company's major business. It is hard to find a place for the conglomerates, which are then seen as holding companies of a portfolio of businesses that have no relationship to one another. Even now, in the '80s there is evidence that the rage to diversify, which swept American business in the '60s and the '70s is largely spent. The present tendency is to consolidate rather than diversify. Exxon is an example, with its rededication to energy as its primary business.

This tendency is a consequence of the evolution of the corporation. Corporations will increasingly concentrate on the provision of a line of related products and services derived from innovation, rather than on a broad range of commodities produced by different business units under a central management. By concentrating rather than diversifying, the corporation strengthens its corporate identity, enhances its expertise and improves its sense of purpose.

Let me give an example from our experience at SmithKline Beckman. We began to diversify in the '60s. In addition to our health businesses, we first moved into ultrasonics (which had certain health care as well as industrial applications) and later, through our merger with Beckman Instruments, we acquired other industrial operations.

As we reviewed our organization in the strategic planning process, however, it became apparent that our greatest gain—and our greatest competency—was associated with our health care businesses, which was the company's focus for a century and a half. Industrial businesses did not fit easily into our culture; nor did we have sufficient management expertise in their administration.

In 1983, we divested ourselves of our industrial businesses.

This transaction enabled the company to devote undivided attention to its primary strategic objective and provided additional resources to strengthen further our already substantial positions in the therapeutic and diagnostic/ analytical fields of health care. Equally important, it facilitated the articulation of a truly integrated health care strategy.

Creating a sharper definition of our business purpose was essential. It was the first step toward bringing our corporate performance closer to the new model of the corporation that I am predicting for the next century and beyond. Since we had business operations in more than 120 countries, we had largely achieved the necessary global perspective. We realized that we also had to undertake structural integration of the organization; and this step raised many questions that authorities on management have long debated.[13] I will touch on some of the principal issues in the ensuing discussion.

CUSTOMER-STIMULATED ORGANIZATION

A fourth point that needs to be made about the new model of the corporation is that the external business environment is the principal stimulus leading to corporate change. The dynamics affecting organizational structure come primarily from without, mainly prompted by changes in technology, in the competitive environment, in human behavior and needs and especially in the demands of world markets. The customer calls the tune.

PROFIT AND CORPORATE LONGEVITY

A very important, but sensitive, fifth point is that corporations will be impelled to concentrate much more than at present on the creation of long-term value. The societies corporations serve will demand that companies demonstrate their ability to contribute to the quality of life, which is what I mean by "creating value."

Peter Drucker had already emphasized the social aspect of the purpose of business in the early '70s:

> Business activity is seen as a necessarily private activity which, for its own good and its own justification, has to strive for the common good and the stated ends of society. Business enterprise is thus seen as local autonomous self-government which, by serving the ends of society, serves its own self-interests and guarantees its own survival.[14]

I say that this point is sensitive because a fairly standard interpretation of the major purpose of the corporation now is that it exists only to make money. But I believe that the purpose of the corporation, and even more the purpose of future corporations, will be to enhance the quality of life through the application of science and technology to the creation of value, a consequence of which is an increase in total world wealth.

Profit, of course, is absolutely necessary to a healthy enterprise because it is the price of the future. Absence of profit is literally the death of a company because it deprives a company of the future. Profit is, in an accounting sense, a forecast of the cash that will be generated by a corporation; as such it is the source of its future capital. It is important not only in and of itself but because every banker, every potential lender or investor judges the future by measuring the present credit worthiness of the corporation. So we need to generate much of our own capital in a way that is sufficiently sound to attract others to provide us with additional capital, either through equity investment or debt, thereby assuring the future.

Second, profit is the means by which our performance is measured in satisfying the needs of society. Society, our customers, will reject or accept the value we place on the products and services we create. And that will show up negatively in the profit-and-loss statement. If we truly create value, we are rewarded by society with profit. In that sense, profit measures our social accountability.

The value-creating role of a corporation is not often discussed in the literature of business economics. The economic paradigm being taught today and used as a basis for public policy is essentially an equation of capital and labor. The dramatic economic contributions of science and innovation have yet to be widely understood. The corporate emphasis must be put on providing goods and services that meet real human needs—needs that are as yet unmet and that can only be met through heavy capital investments in science and purposeful innovation. To create value, we must find solutions to dilemmas that we have not yet resolved. Finding a cure for cancer is an example.

STRUCTURAL INTEGRATION AND DECENTRALIZATION

If these first five points are relevant to the new model of the corporation, and I believe them to be, the corporations of the future will be society-serving, integrated organizations and will be characterized by the fact that the whole is greater than the sum of its parts. Indeed, I would go so far as to say that if the whole is not greater than the sum of its parts in future corporations, then probably everyone is better served if we split a corporation into smaller pieces.

Certainly employees would be better served; they are closer to management in smaller companies than in larger ones. Customers are probably better served by smaller, more responsive organizations. And communities are better served by smaller companies that are sensitive only to local needs. The sole justification for size on the scale of the *Fortune* 200 is to ensure that the whole is greater than the sum of its parts; and that requires the full integration of the corporation. The need for structural integration in the new model of the corporation is my sixth major point, although I have suggested its relevance earlier.

Louis A. Allen made the point well when discussing the relation of corporate divisions to the whole:

Several decades of overdiversification have brought the lesson home, and today there is a general tendency to make the whole enterprise greater than the sum of its divisions by exploiting the potential synergy of complementary products, shared technology, and common sources of supply.[15]

Specifically, what is meant by integration? Let me use R&D as an example. Here integration means that the science and technology bases not only fit the specific business objectives of the division but that they also fit together and support other R&D units within the corporation.

In today's world, ideas and knowledge flow freely; there are no artificial barriers to knowledge. Similarly, within the new model of the corporation, ideas and knowledge are shared by all science-based components, although their products serve different markets.

In the case of SmithKline Beckman, we have a research operation in the United Kingdom that has developed a sophisticated understanding of the effects in the human body of histamine. This operation was responsible for the new discovery of histamine$_2$ receptors. This discovery led us to the development of Tagamet, our antiulcer drug product, which is an antagonist to histamine$_2$ and combats the ulcer-causing buildup of excess acid in the gastrointestinal system.

We also have a business in California engaged in eye care research. This operation is important to our health care objective because an aging population (now characteristic of the demographic pattern in the United States and other developed countries) has an increasing need for eye care products.

We have shared the findings of these two scientific programs. Each synergistically exploits the knowledge of the other in the search for new health care products in which histamine control is of significance.

Another example is the interchange of scientific knowledge between our anti-infective programs in SmithKline Beckman's ethical pharmaceuttcal R&D and the use of antibiotics in the feed additives produced by our animal health business.

These are only two examples of many within our corporation of ways in which shared science and technological knowledge contributes to the development of new products useful in human and animal health.

In the new model of the corporation, then, one should expect that every element will support some or all of the other elements. This exchange is part of what I mean by organic integration, and I do not believe that the corporations of the next hundred years or so can function at a maximal value-creating level without it.

In describing Sony's reorganization to achieve maximum

integration, Shigeru Kobayashi points to the need for avoiding static stereotypes when considering organizational structures:

> Achieving an organization that will meet our specifications calls, in fact, for constant creative action aimed at formulating a pattern for ourselves on the basis of trial and error. What we must avoid under any circumstances is the stabilization of an organization structure through organization charts and rules based on the concept which views organization as a vehicle for directive management, authority, and status. Teamwork is possible only in small groups. Therefore, we had to redesign our large organization as a collection of interlinking small groups.[16]

As we pursue this policy of integration within the corporation, we must deal with the question of centralization and decentralization, a concept that has been discussed for decades. As Peter Drucker and others have suggested, structure follows strategy; and the mode of decentralization is no exception.[17]

It is common for these two organizational formats to be seen as contradictory or, at least, in a state of tension with each other. But the successful corporation of the future will resolve the contradiction. It will no longer be a matter of centralization *versus* decentralization, but of the integration of the two in ways that will improve the productivity of the corporation as a whole; there will be an ebb and flow between the two administrative modalities.

Russell L. Ackoff states the principle involved:

> The centralization-decentralization issue...arises because in corporations that are neither holding companies nor conglomerates managers require coordination and integration. Even in corporations that are aggregations of independently managed businesses, some coordination and integration is required, and a great deal is required within their parts...To do this requires an unconventional concept of organizational structure.[18]

The new model of the corporation must gain the advantages of decentralization with respect to human motivation and rapid decision making while at the same time taking a centralized view of those corporate functions (shared technology may be an example) where knowledge critical to all elements within the corporation must be effectively exchanged.

There will always be a central view of the corporation, but what is centralized and what is decentralized will differ from one business to another, depending on the overall corporate objective. In our case, science, business strategy, finance and human resources, while to some degree decentralized, will be weighted toward centralized control so that we can have a corporate perspective and a capability that enables us to initiate major strategies affecting the course of the enterprise as a whole.

Financial and managerial controls must be flexible. The corporation will have centralized financial and managerial controls, for example, to set clear objectives and measure progress toward them. It will have decentralized controls once an objective is agreed upon, so that the manager determines the method by which he or she meets that objective.

This approach to the classical centralized/decentralized paradox views the tension between the two forms of organization not as contradictory but as complementary. The balance to be achieved is delicate and requires judicious handling by management. It is an attempt to gain the advantages of both centralization and decentralization while minimizing the disadvantages of each.

MOTIVATION

The seventh point in developing a new model of the corporation has to do with the motivation of employees. There are already indications that the concept of "work" is undergoing change.[19],[20]

Management must organize and lead in such a way as to promote optimum motivation. Since most of the large corporations of the future will be rooted in science and technology (at least that is my hypothesis), motivation takes priority over efficiency. Conscious discovery is a creative process, and conscious discovery without motivation is impossible. Nor can creativity be measured on the same scale as efficiency.

The organization must be tuned to promote individual initiative. This concept implies that it is a management responsibility to improve the quality of work life to enhance individual productivity. I emphasize this point because traditional managerial science and much of the literature on management—even the concept of "business" itself—are now directed more toward efficiency enhancement than motivation.

How do we create the climate that stimulates motivation? I suggest four major ingredients for consideration:

First, the purpose, the central objective, of the business has to be understood by all hands. That understanding must go beyond the understanding that a business has to make a profit for shareholders. There must be an understanding of the business unit within the corporation as a whole along with an understanding of the corporation's core purpose.

In the case of SmithKline Beckman, it is well understood by all employees that we are a science- and technology-based corporation dedicated to improving the quality of the life sciences and health care and contributing to the productivity of our customers.

Without that first ingredient, a core purpose understood by all, it is difficult to move on to the succeeding ones that are necessary to improve individual motivation.

The second ingredient is to organize in relatively small units so that people know each other personally and feel close to the leader of the unit.

I sometimes liken the concept of unit smallness to the organization of the British Navy in the late eighteenth and early nineteenth centuries, the age of Admiral Horatio Nelson. By today's standards, the ship units were small, perhaps from 100 to 1,000 people in each. Everyone could see the captain of the ship and hear the orders given directly.

The record of the British Navy in Nelson's time shows consistently the effect of superior leadership and motivation, often with ships that were technically inferior. It is also an interesting analogy of organic organization since great flexibility allowed individual ship actions, all the way to maneuvers of giant fleets, depending, of course, on the objectives and strategy required.

I am aware that I am using a military analogy, and that I

earlier alluded to the inadequacy of military prototypes for the new model of the corporation. As it happens, however, earlier forms of military organization—not those with which we are familiar since the end of the nineteenth century—often employed unit smallness as a device for assuring good communication and coordinated action. The advent of "unlimited war" has seemed to encourage larger units and more difficult control, which has often resulted in a loss of identification with the objectives of a military operation as a whole. The shift of the U.S. Army from large-scale ground combat to completely autonomous small-scale combat units, with sea and air support, is an example of the usefulness of unit smallness and an organic response.

At SmithKline Beckman, our units are small enough to allow people to know one another. They see and hear the captain and develop a common personal bond. In putting the emphasis on small units, I am by no means eliminating the function of admirals and vice admirals, who help set the strategy for the fleet as a whole. But at the unit level, smallness is an asset.

The third ingredient is for people within the organization to have common bonds. These should be both personal and organizational, uniting people as people, not simply as coworkers.

This ingredient is almost intangible; it is an aspect of the corporate culture. It tends to grow out of a common heritage and common experiences. But it also suggests that the managers of the corporation personify the corporate culture and must be chosen selectively.

As Harry A. Bullis anticipated as early as the 1960s, in the introduction to J. D. Batten's book on *Tough-Minded Management*:

> The business executive in the remaining decades of this century and beyond must demonstrate unprecedented leadership—leadership that combines disciplined intellect and faith in the highest ideals. The business manager in a free society belongs to the people.[21]

CORPORATE CULTURE

I have referred to "corporate culture" several times, and it is the eighth important consideration in the new model of the corporation. A good deal has been written about it in books on management,[22] and it is possible that my explanation is redundant. Yet I consider the subject of so much importance that a few additional words about it may not be amiss.

Corporate culture is a social, or even anthropological, term applied to the business organization. It suggests that some of the characteristics familiar to us in social relations may be useful in the corporate setting.

As with families, a common tradition is helpful. Older, tightly knit companies often have this tradition. It is derived in part from the character of the company's founder or founders, to which have been added over the years cultural nuances from other managers of the company who have been successful leaders and have had forceful personalities.

Corporate culture is also a function of management style. SmithKline Beckman has been fortunate in having a long series of corporate leaders who were informal, open, often idiosyncratic and educated in the classical liberal arts and sciences tradition. Almost without exception they had interests in cultural or sporting activities and were socially active. They imparted to the corporation qualities of poise, integrity, common sense, purposefulness and good humor. Their informality and accessibility became characteristic of the organization.

Corporate culture arises, I believe, mainly through shared experience, and in a large corporation largely depends on the quality of internal communications. It is present in inverse proportion to the amount of bureaucracy with which a company is burdened.

Organizational structure is also a positive or negative factor in the development of a corporate culture. I have already mentioned the importance of a small-unit organization. In addition, management must attempt to keep the organization fluid, open to change, although it should not embrace change arbitrarily. Too much change arouses organizational anxiety.

Corporate culture is more qualitative than quantitative. It has an almost esthetic quality that is difficult to define. It is nourished by a corporate philosophy and an ethical impulse that should, under ideal circumstances, radiate from the top down through the entire organization, although the larger the organization, the less likely we are to communicate the philosophy successfully, and ethical imperatives are always subject to the blemishes of misjudgment.

For a cohesive corporate culture, there must be incentives (indeed, a whole system of incentives) that encourage long-term employment, a feeling of job security and a sense of trust in the company's leadership. But at best, the cultivation of a corporate culture is perhaps as irrational as the creation of a successful piece of art.

Lawrence M. Miller, in his analysis of the future corporate culture, identifies eight principles that he believes are essential.[23] He expresses these principles in a few key words: purpose, excellence, consensus, unity, performance, empiricism, intimacy and integrity. He then explains them in detail (with examples) throughout the rest of his book, while at the same time suggesting concrete measures that can be taken to put them into effect. I am in agreement with a great deal of what he recommends, although I think he would agree that the emphasis given to each principle would vary from corporation to corporation.

Finally, I think corporate culture requires management to create a climate that permits failure and rewards success. This climate might be described as one of positive reinforcement. It stimulates motivation because it conforms with human nature, where trial and error are the principal means of acquiring knowledge, and the possibility of failure introduces a risk factor that, seemingly perversely, is essential to success.

The freedom to take risks, to fail or to succeed, is necessary if managers wish to instill motivation and productivity. By giving greater autonomy to smaller units within the corporation, by allowing them to explore functional modes that are not strictly prescribed, we increase personal responsibility and cultivate motivation. This aspect of human behavior, which most of us understand on a common sense level, has not been fully applied to the operations of American corporations.

Indeed, it is a curious anomaly that, while we speak so often of the need for entrepreneurship in our free-market economic system, at the same time we strive to minimize risk-taking with an administrative apparatus designed to produce adherence to defined procedures.

A similar contradiction may be seen on the macro level in discussions of "national industrial policy" and trade protectionism. Both concepts have the intention of minimizing competition and risk-taking. We must accept in corporate life, as well as in our international trade relations, that reality is filled with imbalance, risk and ambiguity; and that far from being destructive to human enterprise, these features of the real world are constructive. All of history demonstrates the inevitability of the tearing down of the old to make way for the creation of the new. Human enterprise, as much as we strive to keep it in balance, is subject to the same forces.

MANAGEMENT LAYERS

The ninth feature of the new model of the corporation concerns the matter of layers of management within an organization. An organic corporation will necessarily have fewer layers than a hierarchical one. The present concepts of the number who should report to a given manager and the manner in which work should be delegated are based on a contemporary administrative understanding of the managerial role. Corporations of the future will undoubtedly modify those concepts.

We can expect the future to bring more responsibility and more recognition to those who perform than to those who merely supervise the performance of others. This concept is encapsulated in the aphorism that responsibility takes precedence over authority. In short, we should be prepared for the hands-on approach to business, in which the task becomes more important than the manager and requires his or her active participation in the work needed to achieve team results.

Close examination of present-day corporations shows that there are often ad hoc situations where lines of authority passing through layers of managers are not strictly observed. Deviations from hierarchical administration occur when higher levels of management need expertise or action at a lower level and communications would be blurred by going through many levels of command.

Although delegation of authority encourages individual initiative, the corporation of the future will demand that it be accompanied by a manager's active participation in task-oriented work. Present concepts of the manager's role are ordinarily viewed as reporting relationships, with the manager acting as a conduit through which information flows.

Hierarchical organizations tend to encourage passivity on the part of managers. In fact, strict hierarchies tend to frown upon managerial participation in work, apparently having in mind the eighteenth- and nineteenth-century distinction between management and labor. This distinction will tend to lose meaning in task-oriented corporate cultures of the future.

If a manager can add nothing creative to the task, he or she may well be expendable. Future corporate organization will be conducted with fewer management levels than at present as the "top" and the "bottom" become more intimately connected. We can therefore expect to see shrinkage in the importance of what we now call middle management.

It has long been a precept of management theory that the span of reporting relationships should be relatively small. The idea that a manager cannot have more than a limited number reporting to him or her leads to the creation of new layers of managers, which in turn leads to bureaucracy. American corporations are especially afflicted with a lack of empiricism on this point. A capable manager should be able to deal effectively with a fairly large number of subordinates. Such relationships formerly were conducted face-to-face, but as a result of information technology, they can now be handled with much less expenditure of personal time. The result of increasing the span of reporting relationships is improvement in communication, motivation and the identification of all employees with the objectives of the corporation.

MYTH AND MANAGEMENT

The tenth aspect of the new model of the corporation will be what I call demythologization of organizational assumptions that are now assumed *a priori*.

Examples of current myths—a few of which I am expressing here in the form of slogans that most American managers will understand—are those of "rugged individualism" (to which I refer later), "authority from the top down," "eternal optimism," "never say no," "quick turnaround," "independent judgment," "fast track" and similar terms that embody a concept of independence, aggression and quick, tough action as norms for acceptable, even successful, management behavior. These myths for the most part are based, probably unconsciously, on the needs of the American frontier society.

In U.S.-based corporations, management mythology can be seen to arise mainly as a result of concepts about the place of the individual in social groups, of which the corporation is but one example. Television and comic strip scenarios exemplify the typical expectations: to be solved, problems must be "exciting" and are usually unraveled by the intervention of a magically potent individual.

The mythology of heroic individual (not team or group) problem solving by a person of extraordinary powers within a short period of time is the unconscious prototype for the charismatic American manager.

In reality, corporate problems are rarely clear cut and "exciting," require considerable time and patience to solve and are better dealt with by small groups who understand the intricacies of a situation than by omnipotent managers who suddenly leap into the breach with a highly original solution.

Fortunately, culturally based mythologies about corporate behavior are gradually undergoing change. This change is particularly evident to those of us with multinational corporations based in the U.S. I attribute the changes in attitudes toward corporate organization and behavior in American corporations to the effect of technology and, beyond that, to the need for humanizing the corporation. The corporate response to technological advance and to humanization is tending to push U.S. corporations toward organizations that resemble other international models.

FLEXIBILITY AND ADAPTABILITY

The response to technology and humanization deserves further attention as we consider future corporate models. This internal response is the eleventh point I would like to make about the corporate model of the future—its flexibility and adaptability.

I remarked earlier that technological change has been largely responsible for the rise of large U.S. corporations. If one traces the origins of America's larger corporations, especially the Fortune 200, I believe that will be found to be the case in most instances.

Changes in technology have an effect upon corporate development similar in many respects to the effect that changes in energy sources have had upon cultures. Thus, there have been wood-burning, coal-burning, oil-burning, electrical and nuclear energy sources, each tending to create a cultural response that has introduced new ways of warfare, manufacturing, dressing, eating, playing and thinking—even philosophies have seemed to be a reflection of changes in a society's use of energy.

In our time, technology is rapidly changing our institutions. It is improbable that information-oriented, computerized technology will leave the corporation untouched.

The second major cause of alterations in management theory is the now apparent need to humanize the corporation as democratic capitalism (Michael Novak's term)[24] competes with socialism for the allegiance of world populations. Socialism has emphasized moral and ethical values, while capitalism has emphasized its efficiency as a productive process and its success in gratifying consumer needs.

Historically, capitalism has been characterized as greedy, self-serving, wasteful of natural resources and unfair in the sense that it benefits the owners of the means of production to a greater degree than it benefits consumers. Socialism, on the other hand, holds that the means of production should be owned by the government and the benefits of that ownership should be shared equally by all citizens.

In practice, as everyone (including capitalists and socialists) knows, neither of these characterizations is accurate. Socialism has become a form of state capitalism and capitalism in nonsocialist countries is hedged about by government with quasi-socialist regulations.

Nevertheless, corporations are, and I think properly, responding to world expectations by introducing more humanistic internal practices and emphasizing ethical and moral values in their planning and performance, including marketing. In my judgment, this emphasis will continue and will increase. Corporations today are still in transition. In the twenty-first century and beyond, values will be central in corporate decision making about both internal and external policies.

A BALANCE OF CONSENSUS, REVIEW AND RESPONSIBILITY

My view is that values can best be inculcated in an organization through the proper balance between the elements of consensus, review and the exercise of responsibility. This balance is the twelfth characteristic that I expect to see in the new model of the corporation.

Consensus is much talked about in Japanese corporate models, where it plays virtually a central role in administrative procedure. As a concept for stimulating action (which I consider it should be), it is rarely given a prominent place in hierarchical models, except perhaps in small committees or groups of officers at the apex of the corporate pyramid. Yet it is a process in the tradition of the New England town meetings, as contrasted with the rugged individualism of the frontier society.

Consensus can take many forms, ranging from a democratic vote with a majority prevailing to total agreement by all participants in a group. Usually it means a team approach to a strategy or a tactic in which the group explores all of the variables, arriving finally at a general agreement by most participants, although there may be minority dissent, as to the best course of action. The administrative virtue of consensus is that it gives employees a stake in decision making, enables them to identify with the decisions reached and, in the best of worlds, may uncover new entrepreneurial ideas.

Review is the sharing of a manager's decision with others in his group or with others in different groups who have an interest in or knowledge of the subject. It is a process of testing; experience shows that review may often result in modification of the original idea to the advantage of the organization. Like consensus, review has as its premise the possibility that individuals can err in judgments and that two or more minds are better than one. Both consensus and review are the denial of the myth of rugged individualism.

There is a time, however, for using what might be called "ultimate responsibility" in making decisions; these are generally short-term operating decisions with less than strategic consequences. Most are made quickly and concern crisis situations in which delay is impossible.

What is the role of the CEO in this model where consensus, small unit decision making and decentralization of responsibility are the norm? The CEO articulates a corporate vision, provides direction, motivates and causes others to motivate, reconciles conflict, personifies the corporate culture and rewards. He or she is at the nucleus of the living organism of the corporation and is the regulator of its metabolism.

Taken together, these decisions—especially those made by consensus—determine corporate strategy and ultimately define the system of values that will prevail in the organization.

WHAT WILL THE FUTURE HOLD?

In summary, the Fortune 200 of the long-term future will almost certainly be different from today's list. One of the great social virtues of private enterprise is that companies can go bankrupt. Government institutions, on the other hand, may continue to exist long after they have a use. State-owned companies in several developed countries show a similar lack of responsiveness to real economic forces. The tentative quality of the corporation keeps it pliable; it also suggests a future for the corporation that is largely unpredictable.

Before summarizing the handful of principles that I believe will be characteristic of corporations in the long-term future, it would perhaps be wise to observe with considerable emphasis that adaptation is easier to describe than to implement. Bookstores are crammed with volumes on management technique, but both managers and organizations have great difficulty in accepting a new and at first generally uncomfortable replacement for the status quo. There is always stubborn resistance to change.

Such resistance is as characteristic of human nature as it is of corporations. Change creates unease. Managers attempting to bring about change may be frustrated by a curious feature of bureaucracy that I have often observed, especially in government, although it is seen in business organizations as well. It is the virtual refusal to change, a kind of quasi-insubordination, despite administrative imperatives.

In government, incumbents under Civil Service can resist change because their job security is protected and the possibility of political change every four years may soon invalidate current directives. Organizational resistance to change is less prevalent in business but does occur at the middle and lower managerial levels when there is loss of identification with overall corporate objectives.

Ackoff notes two ways in which organizations often resist change: by making unnecessary work appear to be necessary and by evading measurement of performance. He adds that in conventionally organized corporations, resistance to change is more likely to occur than in those that provide strong identification with the objectives of management.[25]

In my opinion, resistance to change is primarily a function of poor internal communication, inadequate personal involvement of lower management levels in corporate planning and lack of integration in the structure of the organization.

A few general principles about corporations of the future can now be hypothesized:

The corporation as an institution is sounder structurally than almost any other institution on the planet—not excluding churches and governments—because it can respond rapidly to social and environmental change. Corporations will continue to exist.

Corporations are bound to technology. Most have been created by technological breakthroughs and will change as technology changes.

The organizational patterns of corporations will reflect the products or services they sell, the increasing internationalization of production and trade and the demands of population groups.

As corporations adapt to technological and social change, and strive to maintain profitability, they will be forced to accept new, perhaps radical, changes in corporate strategies, styles and structures. The general trend will be toward specialization in corporate purpose, organic integration in organization and deployment of human resources in novel ways to promote motivation and productivity.

Standard hierarchical patterns of organization (those with which we are familiar today) will give way to variations adapted to specific market demands; these will evolve in response to circumstances that may not yet be predictable.

Corporate survivors in the future will be characterized by maximum flexibility, great sensitivity to basic human needs and the capacity for discovering rapid and innovative solutions to the demands of highly varied world markets.

REFERENCES

1. Peter F. Drucker, *The Concept of the Corporation* (New York: John Day, 1946).
2. Hugh Thomas, *A History of the World* (New York: Harper & Row, 1979), pp. 422 ff.
3. Ibid. p. 424.
4. Thomas J. Peters and Robert H. Waterman, Jr., *In Search of Excellence* (New York: Harper & Row, 1982).
5. Ruth Gilbert Shaeffer, *Developing Strategic Leadership*, Report No. 847 (The Conference Board, 1984).
6. Ibid, p. 5.
7. Peter F. Drucker, *The Age of Discontinuity* (New York: Harper & Row, 1968, 1969).
8. Robert G. Eccles, "Creating the Collaborative Organization," in *Course Development & Research Profile, 1984* (Boston: Harvard Business School, 1984), p. 75.
9. William I. Gordon, "Organizational Imperatives and Cultural Modifiers," *Business Horizons* 27 (May-June, 1984), p. 76.
10. Ibid., p. 80.
11. Ibid.
12. William Ouchi, *Theory Z* (Reading, Mass.: Addison-Wesley, 1981).
13. A good survey of organizational systems, making many useful points, is Russell L. Ackoff, *Creating the Corporate Future* (New York: John Wiley & Sons, 1981).
14. Peter F. Drucker, *Men, Ideas & Politics* (New York: Harper & Row, 1971), p. 178.
15. Louis A. Allen, *Making Managerial Planning More Effective* (New York: McGraw-Hill, 1982), p. 95.
16. Shigeru Kobayashi, *Creative Management* (New York: American Management Association, Inc., 1971), pp. 129-30.
17. Peter F. Drucker, *Management* (New York: Harper & Row, 1973), p. 523. Mr. Drucker credits Alfred D. Chandler with development of the original idea in his book *Strategy and Structure* (Cambridge, Mass. MIT Press, 1962).

18. Ackoff, *Creating the Corporate Future*, p. 152.
19. Isaac Asimov et al, *Work in the 21st Century* (Alexandria, Va.: The American Society for Personnel Administration, 1984).
20. Robert Levering, Milton Moskowitz, and Michael Katz, *The 100 Best Companies to Work for in America* (Reading, Mass.: Addison-Wesley, 1984).
21. J.D. Batten, *Tough-Minded Management* (New York: American Management Association, Inc., 1963), p. 5.
22. An interesting recent contribution is: Lawrence M. Miller, *American Spirit Visions of a New Corporate Culture* (New York: William Morrow and Company, 1984). Miller seems to have a good grasp of many of the principles I am describing in this chapter.
23. Ibid, p. 15 ff.
24. Michael Novak, *The Spirit of Democratic Capitalism* (New York: American Enterprise Institute/Simon and Schuster, 1982).
25. Ackoff, *Creating the Corporate Future*, p. 152.

Robert Anderson

Robert Anderson, chairman of the board and chief executive officer of Rockwell International Corporation, was elected chairman in 1979, after serving nine years as president. He has been chief executive officer since 1974.

He joined Rockwell in 1968, after 22 years with Chrysler Corporation, where he rose to the post of vice-president and general manager of the Chrysler-Plymouth Division.

A graduate of Colorado State University with a bachelor's degree in mechanical engineering, Mr. Anderson also received a master's degree in automotive engineering from the Chrysler Institute of Engineering.

Mr. Anderson is a recipient of awards and honors for his civic and business activities, including the National Management Association's Executive of the Year Award in 1980, the Executive of the Year Award in 1982, the University of California at Los Angeles Executive Program Association's Executive of the Year Award and, in 1983, *Financial World* magazine named him outstanding chief executive of the year in the aerospace industry. He was appointed by President Reagan as National United Nations' Day chairman for both 1981 and 1982—the only man ever to hold that post more than once.

In 1984 Mr. Anderson concluded a two-year term as chairman of the Business-Higher Education Forum, comprising heads of major U.S. corporations and universities. He also served as co-chairman of a Forum task force that studied the issue of American competitiveness.

President Reagan appointed him in 1983 to the Presidential

Commission on Industrial Competitiveness, a panel of 21 business, labor and academic leaders who recommended solutions to improve America's competitiveness in the world marketplace.

2
MANAGING
DIVERSIFICATION
By Robert Anderson
Chairman and Chief Executive Officer
Rockwell International Corporation

Managing a diversified industrial company is one of the most challenging, and potentially one of the most rewarding, jobs in the business world. For Rockwell, managing diversification effectively accounts as much for our future as it has for our present.

I speak from experience. When I am asked to describe some of the complexities of managing a company that makes everything from printing presses to the space shuttle orbiter, I sometimes compare it to the role of a pilot flying a plane.

Again, I speak from experience. When I joined Rockwell in 1968, I had a background of 22 years as an engineer and executive in the automotive industry. Automotive components were an important part of Rockwell's business—and still are. But another major Rockwell business area was aerospace, the development and manufacture of aircraft, rockets and manned space vehicles.

Shortly after I came to Rockwell, I began to take flying lessons and eventually earned my pilot's license. I did it, in part, as a way of better understanding some of the basics of the aerospace business. And I found it a pleasurable hobby. But the surprising thing for me was how much flying had in common with my down-to-earth job, managing a diversified, multi-industry company.

In flying, the pilot controls complex systems that must work together harmoniously. The pilot monitors multiple sources of information—radar, messages from the tower, and all the various dials, gauges and electronic readouts in the cockpit—and then uses that information to make decisions that are vital to the safety and success of the flight. It is not just a one-person job. It involves a great deal of teamwork with ground control, and an acute awareness of the external factors that can affect the flight.

Many of the same kinds of decisions that a pilot makes also take place in the day-to-day operation of a company. Management oversees and directs the varied systems and organizations within the different business areas. Information gathering is important, too. Just as the pilot needs to know the weather conditions and the location of other aircraft, so does company management need to be aware of the competitive business climate and the actions of its business rivals.

The business manager's job is a complex one. That is true to a large extent in any company, but it is especially the case in high-tech, multi-industry companies.

Our experiences at Rockwell are a good example of some of the benefits and problems to be derived from business diversification.

THE ROCKWELL GROUP

Rockwell comprises four businesses.

One is aerospace. We develop and manufacture military aircraft, manned and unmanned space systems, rocket engines, advanced space-based surveillance systems, and high-energy laser and other directed-energy programs.

Our electronics business serves both the commercial and defense markets in various areas, including precision guidance and control; tactical weapons; command, control, communications and intelligence; precision navigation; avionics; telecommunications; and semiconductors.

Our automotive business manufactures axles, brakes and other components for medium- and heavy-duty trucks, trailers, buses and off-highway equipment, as well as components for passenger cars and light-duty trucks.

Rockwell's fourth business area, General Industries, produces printing presses; valves, meters and other flow control and measurement equipment for energy markets; and industrial sewing machines. It also engages in nuclear-related work for the U.S. government.

These four basic business areas represent a broad variety of markets, affected by different business and economic cycles. They are a mixture of commercial businesses and government contracting, each with its own set of problems, opportunities and rewards.

This did not happen by accident. The company, as constituted today, has taken shape since the mid-1970s. The lessons learned along the way illustrate some of the strengths and potential weaknesses of diversification, and how management decisions can make the difference between the two.

At Rockwell, we have gone through an era of rapid expansion, followed by a period of asset redeployment, and, finally, our current period of strong but steady growth.

We have shaped a company that has grown from $4 billion to more than $9 billion in sales over the past decade, and we have earned the less tangible rewards that come from applying advanced technology to a wide range of business areas.

Rockwell International evolved out of a 1967 merger between North American Aviation, a major aerospace manufacturer, and Rockwell-Standard Corporation, an automotive components producer. That merger formed North American Rockwell Corporation and was the basis for further mergers and acquisitions.

It was in this period of the late '60s and early '70s that American industry passed through what has been called the "go-go years." It was a time when an atmosphere of exhilaration swept through the stock markets and the board rooms. Many companies forged ahead with acquisitions and mergers on a broad front. They paid for these transactions with paper and often piled together unrelated businesses, concentrating on what was perceived as growth, and confident that such growth could be managed and sustained somehow in the years ahead.

Rockwell was in the thick of all this activity, and grew rapidly. By 1974 we had folded in Rockwell Manufacturing, a producer of valves and water and gas meters; Collins Radio, a leading electronics company; Admiral, a maker of television sets and appliances; and a number of smaller companies. And we changed our name from North American Rockwell to Rockwell International.

MANAGEMENT CHALLENGE

Our rapid spurt of growth resulted in some Herculean management challenges.

The first was to develop a philosophy that would allow us to assemble the different parts of our new company into a logical and manageable whole, forging them into an entity stronger than any of those constituent parts might have been if left to themselves.

Part of the challenge was to arrive at the best way of managing this collection of diverse businesses. Many had operated for years as independent companies and in the process had developed their own business philosophies and cultures. Because they were in widely varied industries, many also had different ways of doing business and their own accounting methods and terminologies.

Our task was to broaden the professionalism and sophistication of the management approach without snuffing out the entrepreneurial spirit within each of these businesses. We sought to build on existing systems by sharpening budgeting, planning and operating procedures, and developing our managers' strategic thinking and planning abilities. We also had to install a higher level of cost consciousness and bring all the different reporting methods onto common ground.

Although the process of improving reporting and financial controls had begun in the early '70s, it came to a head in 1974. In that year, we faced a debt-to-equity ratio of almost 100 percent and our cash position was deteriorating daily. In fact, at one point we had a negative cash flow of a million dollars a day.

Action was needed, and quickly. We instituted and

enforced centralized cash management. We concentrated attention on inventories and receivables.

Gradually, the situation improved. By the end of the next year, even with higher sales, receivables and inventories declined, and the debt-to-equity ratio improved to 68 percent.

Since then, we have weathered not only our own 1974 "recession" but two major national recessions and many individual up and down cycles in various businesses.

Our experiences in the early '70s taught us some valuable lessons and helped us develop the set of principles that guide us in the way we manage.

Every responsible—and responsive—management team should be concerned about planning and shaping the future of its company through a set of guiding principles; some call it a management philosophy. Such principles are the basis for both short- and long-term success. Certainly, short-term performance is important, but it is more important to identify future trends, then set goals and initiate actions that will ensure that the company takes full advantage of these trends in commerce and technology as they develop.

Rockwell's particular circumstances may be unique, but the rules that we manage by are applicable to many different management situations. The most basic of these principles is strong financial management.

The traumatic debt-to-equity crunch we experienced in 1974 reinforced our determination to adhere to sound and prudent financial management. Like Scarlett O'Hara, we vowed we would never be poor again. And we were successful. In 1984, for example, we had a debt-to-equity ratio of 11 percent and more than a billion dollars in cash.

Our early exposure to turbulence also helped us to focus on some other basic attributes of the company. Our management agreed that we were not a holding company, managing our business as a financial portfolio. And we were not a conglomerate, entering any business without regard for its relationship to our other businesses or our management skills. Instead, we positioned ourselves as an operating company, a diversified manufacturing company in high-technology businesses.

Most of our business areas share certain common denominators. They hold a strong leadership position in their markets. They are businesses that we understand, and in which we have established a proven track record. And these diverse businesses are tied together by a unifying bond of advanced technology, applied to materials and process research on a wide variety of products.

We are known as the company "where science gets down to business," a phrase we adopted as our corporate slogan.

But competition in science and technology is swift and intense, and a company must be a market leader to be successful. Consequently, we decided we could succeed by building our strategies around those of our businesses that were leaders in their markets. This is where our growth has been and will continue to be—in the areas we know best.

We went through a long appraisal and analysis of all our businesses in regard to the competition each faced, their market share, and the future potential. Where we saw that we could not be among the leaders in a market, we withdrew, and we withdrew from a lot of markets.

If we cannot be in a strong leadership position in the market, or see a way to get that position in a reasonably short period of time, with a reasonable expenditure of money, then we would rather put our money and our energy to work elsewhere—in business areas where we can utilize our strengths and get the return on sales, investment and equity that a leader can expect.

This philosophy launched a period of asset redeployment for the company, when we pruned away some of our business areas. In just five years—1978 through 1982—Rockwell divested or discontinued businesses with total sales of over a billion dollars. Yet our core businesses continued to push the company's total sales volume upward, in steady, stable growth, and they generated nine straight years of improved earnings through 1984.

We understood what we were and where we were going, and this knowledge sustained the company even when turbulent times threatened the equilibrium of the worldwide business climate.

In 1983 and 1984, once again the business community saw a repeat of the "go-go years" in terms of a tremendous number of mergers that were tremendous in dollar volume as well. Felix Rohatyn, senior partner at Lazard Freres & Co., told the *Washington Post* in late 1984, "I lived through the go-go years of the 1960s, but the last couple of years makes the go-go years look like Little Lord Fauntleroy."

But, at Rockwell, we took what we considered a balanced approach. Rockwell's recent business growth, both internal and through acquisitions, has been geared toward strengthening our core businesses in gradual increments, not taking on a new line of business merely to give sales and earnings a quick shot in the arm. Although I advocate the virtues of diversification, I also preach moderation. Unlimited diversification can be worse than no diversification at all. The goal of diversification should be not merely short-term improvement, but rather long-term growth and success.

THE LIMITS OF OPTIMAL DIVERSIFICATION

How much diversification is enough? And how much is too much? Unfortunately, there is no golden mean when it comes to planning your business mix.

For us at Rockwell, our concentration on core businesses does not mean that we have put all our eggs in one basket. By providing a mix of business, between government and commercial markets, and among different segments within those markets, diversity has been enhanced. This has helped the company maintain a steady course through the peaks and valleys of individual market cycles.

Overall, we believe that our diversification has proved its worth in the past few years. For example, our automotive business was our biggest profit contributor back in 1979, a time when our government business was at a low ebb. However, when the automotive business hit bottom in the early '80s, the government business had recovered and helped us keep our corporate profits growing.

Profits from a strong business area can be used to invest in another business which has good potential but is in a temporary slump. We invested heavily in our automotive business during its down cycle to modernize plants and equipment and innovate new products. We lowered our costs, and, at the same time, improved the quality of our products.

The result was seen in 1984 when our automotive business earned more than in 1979, its previous best year, even though

industry sales volume in our important truck markets was 35
percent below the record levels of 1979. In 1984, North
American heavy-duty truck sales were 153,000, compared
with 216,000 in 1979. And medium-duty truck sales were
147,000 units, compared with 266,000 in 1979.

We also have learned that, while a mix of businesses is
important, more important is the ability to improve profits no
matter which way the balance might shift.

In our diversification planning, we try to strike a balance in
the ratio of our government and commercial business. In the
mid-1980s, due to some large government contracts such as
the B-1B, the balance has tipped to the government side.

We are not too concerned about the exact proportion of
government versus commercial, but we do plan to maintain
diversity. Other companies also have found a multi-industry
approach serves them well, certainly in good economic
conditions, but also in hard times. A *Fortune* magazine study
showed that, since 1980, diversified companies produced a
higher   median   return   on   shareholders'   equity   than
nondiversified   companies.   The   contrast   was   especially
obvious in the recession year of 1982.

This is a key reason why I believe diversification is one of
the important business trends in the next few years. I do not
foresee a return to the heyday of conglomerates, but even
modest diversification can give a business a great advantage in
the marketplace. It makes for a more stable company, steadier
growth, and sales and profits that are more cycle-resistant. It
means putting all of your eggs in several baskets.

CONSIDERATIONS FOR THE FUTURE

Diversification is only one of the coming trends for which
business professionals must be prepared. Another of these
trends is the streamlining of management structure.

Today, most forward-looking companies are developing a
leaner orginization chart, peeling away cumbersome layers of
management and thereby allowing quicker response time on
important issues. Decision-making authority is being pushed
down to the lowest practical level on the hierarchical ladder.

And companies are learning to get along with fewer people.

A survey by Louis Harris & Associates found, as might be expected, that more than 40 percent of 1,200 major companies made cuts in their middle-management staffs in the 1982 recession year. This included a large proportion of major, across-the-board personnel reductions.

But the more revealing statistic from this survey was that management at nearly two-thirds of these companies said the reductions actually had increased productivity.

This does not necessarily mean that the original organization was bloated with superfluous people doing unnecessary work. It simply means that there were better, easier and faster ways to accomplish the same corporate goals by taking a fresh look at the way the management function operates.

Other changes are taking place in the way companies deal with their employees. Through quality circles, suggestion programs and other channels, companies are encouraging employees at all levels—white and blue collar, hourly and salaried—to help find better ways of doing things.

Statistical process control is another means by which employees are encouraged—required, in fact—to take charge of their own decision making. This is a manufacturing program in which a machine operator is responsible for seeing that the parts being produced fall within acceptable quality parameters. It restores basic responsibility where it belongs—at the place and time of product creation.

At Rockwell, we have thousands of workers trained in statistical process control, and similar programs are being used by major industrial companies across the nation.

Flexibility in the management organization is another trend that is being encouraged by bellweather companies today. The soundness of this approach has been proven during a period of corporate growth in a rapidly changing environment. Business is operating in conditions that are far from static, so why should corporate management policies be cast in concrete? In fact, one hallmark of good management is the ability to alter management concepts and to change the way a business is run, as conditions change.

The potential for improvements through reorganization and change should not be limited to mid-level management. Top management also can benefit from new ways of operating.

We have been successful in a major move of this type at Rockwell. To give top management more flexibility, we established an Office of the Chief Executive early in 1982.

I would not prescribe such an arrangement for every company, not even every diversified company. I can only say that, in our case, it has been a very effective way of managing a large and complex organization.

There are three members of Rockwell's Office of the Chief Executive. Joining me are Donald R. Beall, president and chief operating officer; and Martin D. Walker, executive vice-president. This spreads executive and operating responsibilities more evenly among three individuals and improves communication among them. The corporate staff reports to me but serves all the members of my office.

There is also a corporate management committee. It consists of the three members of the office of the chairman, the senior vice-presidents in charge of various staff functions, and our operations presidents. This group meets once a month and reviews staff and line management performance.

Top management follows closely the progress of our major company projects. The members of the office of the chief executive meet quarterly with the heads of each of our major operations to review all of these businesses. These meetings are two-way sessions, in which we get information and recommendations and give a measure of advice and direction.

These are not usually strategy sessions but deal mainly with current operating issues. We have given the individual business segments a primary responsibility for their own strategic planning. There is periodic corporate review and input, and long-range strategy meetings are held on a regularly scheduled basis.

Our goal is not to impose business strategies from the top level down, but for individual businesses to lay plans that are ambitious, yet do-able, and then follow through on them. We expect the people running these operations to accept full responsibility, and we provide the money and the human resources talent necessary to support them.

We encourage what we call entrepreneurship—making bold plans, backing them up and carrying them out. Sometimes that means making mistakes as well, and learning from them.

We rely on our managers for their extensive and intensive knowledge of their individual markets, as well as general management excellence. We encourage them to act like entrepreneurs in the way they plan and invest and market their products and services, and we try to give them as much latitude to act as we can.

This kind of entrepreneurship is another of the trends that will continue to change the American business world. It is not a new idea by any means, but it seems to be acquiring renewed vigor today. We are seeing new companies being formed and thousands of new jobs being created—all based on one person's good idea, a little financing and a lot of enterprise. And, even in large and well-established companies such as Rockwell, the spirit of entrepreneurship is being encouraged.

The entrepreneurial approach is important not only to individual businesses but also to American business as a whole. It can be one of our nation's great strengths in the international competitiveness battle.

This internationalization of business is another trend for which management must be prepared. In past years, there was a concern by many nations around the world that American multinational companies would come to dominate world trade. Today, the tide of foreign trade has swept the other way, with the United States being swamped by imported goods.

American companies are attempting to meet this competition in various ways: by automation, cost cutting and the manufacturing and marketing of products off-shore.

Statistics of the past few years show a strong need for such actions. For example, the United States had a merchandise trade deficit for all but two of the years from 1968 through 1984. The President's Commission on Industrial Competitiveness—on which I served—reported in 1984 that this trade deficit "makes it very difficult for the U.S. to maintain its free trade stance and leads to protectionist remedies that will damage our long-term ability to compete." It is obvious that industrial competitiveness, on a global scale, is crucial to our society and our economy.

One of the most disturbing aspects of our falling trade competitiveness, as the Commission noted, was the decline in our high-technology trade surplus. In the past, our comparative advantage in high-technology goods made up for our deficits in other goods and services. But the high-tech surplus has been dropping since 1980. In 1983 it dropped 23 percent from the previous year—from $22 billion to $17 billion-reflecting stagnation   in   export   growth   and   rapid increase in imports, especially of communications equipment and electronic components.

The composition of our trade balance is important, and we should be particularly concerned at the challenge to our technological leadership. Technology has far greater benefits to the nation than the dollar value of its trade, for, as the Commission described it, technology "is the key to our. productivity growth and the creation of new industries for which it serves as base. If we lose our place in the first round of innovation, it is most difficult to close the gap. Innovation is cumulative in nature and pervasive in its benefits."

Although the United States still has the largest share of world trade, others are catching up. We are facing a strong competitive threat from nations around the world—not just our historic trading partners but newly industrialized countries, as well. For example, although the Japanese have been impressive leaders in productivity, new manufacturing techniques,   and   improved   methods   of   industrial management, today there are "new Japans" entering the field, a second tier of rising industrial nations that have pushed ahead rapidly in business areas such as steel, shipbuilding, machine tools, construction and electronics.

The Department of Commerce reported that American imports from six newly industrialized countries—Mexico, Taiwan, Korea, Hong Kong, Brazil and Singapore—grew by 25 percent in just two years, from 1981 to 1983.

Competitiveness is a large and complex issue which will continue to challenge American business managers, educators and government leaders for years to come. The key action that is needed is for all segments of American society to work together on solutions—in the workplace, the schools and the halls of government—to make the nation more highly competitive in the expanding area of international business.

As   the   President's   Commission   on   Industrial Competitiveness pointed out, "Our challenge is to build on our strengths—our large market, technology base, skilled and flexible work force, and our entrepreneurial culture. At the same time, we must be working toward free and fair international trade."

There is one more trend that is influencing the future direction of business management, and it is one that has become very evident and very pervasive in our lives, even today; it is the large and growing influence of computer technology.

The computer is helping to design our products, manufacture and test them, warehouse, ship and deliver them. And in the office environment, the electronic age is giving us ever-increasing capabilities to plan, forecast and hypothesize our business outlook.

This is happening not just in high-tech businesses, but in traditional business as well. As managers, we must understand and utilize the latest technologies, and be able to apply them to our changing business needs. This may seem obvious for sophisticated projects such as the space shuttle, but it is equally true in more prosaic business activities. We're seeing the tip of this technological iceberg every day in uses such as retail stores where electronic cash registers keep track of inventory as they ring up the customer's purchases.

The problem for management today regarding computers is not how to use them, but how to avoid misusing them. The computer's awesome power has become such a fixture of American business operations that we sometimes run the danger of being used by it, instead of using it.

All of us in business must treat computers as the useful management tool they are, and not as a form of management itself.

Certainly technology has changed the face of business; management must change also. As managers, we must use all the methods at our command—brainpower as well as computer power—to guide our businesses in the direction we would have them go.

Each company, whether diversified or single-business, must develop a management philosophy to meet its own needs and the future trends it perceives. There is no one correct way to manage, because various styles have developed in response to the internal and external pressures that are unique to each company. This does not mean that we cannot learn from one another, our business competitors as well as our partners, but that we need to rely on our own common sense in applying and adapting management solutions to our individual situation.

As General George Patton once said, "Never tell people how to do things. Tell them *what* to do and they will surprise you with their ingenuity."

It is that indigenous American ingenuity that we need to encourage in all our business activities.

Charles L. Brown

Charles L. Brown has been chairman of the American Telephone and Telegraph Company since February 1979—a period of momentous change for the telecommunications industry in general and AT&T in particular.

As the company's chief executive, Mr. Brown has led AT&T through what was the largest corporate reorganization in history, culminating in January 1984 with the divestiture of the local Bell telephone companies. Now he is directing AT&T's efforts to become a worldwide leader in providing Information Age products and services.

Mr. Brown graduated from the University of Virginia in 1943 with a degree in electrical engineering. He then entered the U.S. Navy and served in the Pacific Theater aboard the U.S.S. *Mississippi*.

Upon his discharge in 1946, with the rank of lieutenant, he joined the AT&T Long Lines Department in Hartford, Connecticut, and rose rapidly, holding a series of management positions of increasing responsibility in a number of cities. In 1963 he joined Illinois Bell as a vice-president and general manager, and six years later was elected president of the company. He became an executive vice-president of AT&T in 1974; vice-chairman of the board and chief financial officer in 1976; and president in 1977.

A trustee of the Aspen Institute, Columbia Presbyterian Hospital, the Institute for Advanced Study and the Colonial Williamsburg Foundation, Mr. Brown is also vice-chairman of the Corporate Fund for the John F. Kennedy Center for the Performing Arts in Washington, D.C., and has helped organize support for a number of other civic and charitable organizations. He is a member of the Business Council, of which he was vice-chairman for two years, and of The Business Roundtable.

Mr. Brown is a director of E.I. du Pont de Nemours & Co., Chemical Bank and Chemical New York Corporation and the General Foods Corporation.

3
THE RESHAPING
OF AT&T

By Charles L. Brown
Chairman of the Board
American Telephone and Telegraph Company

When I took office as chairman of AT&T in February 1979, I could scarcely have imagined the development of circumstances that just about three years later would have me standing side by side with Assistant U.S. Attorney General Baxter at the National Press Club in Washington, announcing that I had acceded to the government's proposal to break up the Bell System.

It was never my intention to preside over the demise of the Bell System—and I said as much in numerous speeches after first taking office. At the same time, I did come to the job with what I called at the time a sense of "new realism," a sense that the Bell System had to recognize the world the way it is, not the way we would like it to be, and adapt to it. In fact, I went so far as to say that the Bell System was ready to consider alternate futures. But the ultimate turn of events exceeded the range of alternatives I had had in mind.

What was clear to me, as I assumed office, was that the Bell System was being crippled by uncertainty about its future and the future of the telecommunications industry by the concurrent and conflicting deliberations over telecommunications policy and the structure of the Bell System that were underway in the regulatory, the legislative and the judicial arenas. My first priority was to find a consensus and gain resolution of the issues so the Bell System could get on with planning and managing its business. I also felt as a new chairman I might be, at least for a time, in a position to negotiate and conciliate. Though I had served as president of AT&T since 1977, I was not personally identified with any entrenched positions. In a sense, I might enjoy something akin to the "hundred days of grace" usually accorded new presidents of the United States.

It will no doubt take the distance of historical perspective to understand fully what really led to the dismantling of the Bell System and whether or not the decision to accept the Consent Decree will prove to be, as I said at the press conference, "an alternative which meets the relevant tests of the public interest." And it's clearly too soon to know the full impact this dismantling will have on the future of AT&T.

In these pages, I intend to examine briefly the forces that led to a radical overhaul of the nation's telecommunications structure. I will discuss some of the considerations that led to the organizational form in which AT&T and the Bell companies operate today. And I will look at the likely progress our industry—the information industry—will make in the years ahead as it propels the nation and the world into the Information Age.

Agreeing to the breakup of the Bell System was fundamentally different from any business decision I ever had to make—and the most painful. I grew up in this business, as did my mother and father. Over the course of four decades I held jobs that ranged from digging cable ditches to running operations departments, to handling finances, jobs in virtually every organizational part of the old Bell System. My coworkers and I all felt special about the work we did. It was part business, part family, part institution. Periodic internal squabbles notwithstanding, we knew we provided an essential service to the nation and we took that responsibility seriously. We felt "anointed." And the Bell System was, in our mind, as immortal as the Rockies.

That I was party to its fragmentation, its fall from what it always seemed to be, was less than a good feeling. I knew Bell System people throughout the country would be shocked. They would feel robbed of their very identity. And they took it hard, which, I suppose, underscores that some business decisions are not simply reducible to data you pump through a computer. They have human, flesh-and-blood dimensions; you know you are affecting the lives of scores of people—in our case, a million employees.

Such a realization made it difficult indeed to accept the government's divestiture proposal.

On the other hand, it had become apparent that the Bell System and our entire industry were overdue for change, radical change. For decades we had operated under circumstances that were now being drastically altered by new technology and by public policy decisions that opened the industry to competition.

In retrospect, we can see that these technological advances, which came gradually and with little wide appreciation for their implications, set the stage for subsequent public policy decisions promoting competition. In essence, the new technology helped remove obstacles that previously prevented other companies from even considering entry into the telecommunications business.

Until the '40's, for example, virtually the only practical way of transmitting telephone calls over long distances was through the pairs of copper wire enclosed in cable as thick as a man's arm. The cable had to be strung on poles or buried in the ground and had to span barriers of every description—rivers, mountains, deserts, forests. To enter the business, a newcomer would have had to risk huge sums in acquiring rights of way and physically installing the cable, a task that had taken AT&T decades to complete.

Although it was not immediately apparent, the advent of microwave radio transmission of telephone calls, which Bell Laboratories pioneered during World War II, proved to be a turning point. This technology eliminated the need to procure extensive rights of way and costly aerial or buried cable for long distance service. Using relay towers spaced every 20 to 40 miles or so, the systems were easier to install and maintain than cable, and held the promise, which they soon fulfilled, of cutting costs substantially.

The development of solid-state electronics that began with Bell Laboratories' invention of the transistor in 1947 also hastened the arrival of competition in telecommunications.

Among other things, solid-state electronics made possible communications satellites, "microwave systems in the sky," that represented another significant advance in transmission technology and made the long distance business even more attractive to competitors. The first international communications satellite, AT&T's Telstar, was launched into orbit in 1962.

Of course, solid-state electronics also provided the foundation for the tremendous growth of the computer industry over the last two decades, and in turn created a burgeoning demand for data communications. Indeed, coupled with the advent of microwave technology, that demand provided a strong impetus for new companies to enter the long distance business.

Solid-state electronics also began blurring the distinction between computers and communications. The same silicon chips that run a computer can also run an office communications system (or PBX). As a result, providing commercial communications systems has become an intensely competitive business.

Once it was possible for other companies to provide telecommunications equipment and services, they increasingly sought and obtained permission from the Federal Communications Commission to do so.

The telephone industry, both AT&T and the independently owned telephone companies, reacted warily. We were primarily concerned about the unintended effects that competition would have on traditional rate structures and the accompanying impact on our customers and operations. Over the years, telephone rates had been carefully designed to achieve both social and economic objectives, such as nationwide averaging of long distance rates and the use of long distance revenues to subsidize local telephone rates. The industry, including AT&T, the major independent telephone systems and the small telephone companies, argued that while competition might benefit some customers, it would ultimately mean higher prices and less convenience for others.

In any event, AT&T urged that if there was to be competition, it should be full and fair competition, with the same ground rules for all competitors. But just the opposite occurred. Every decision that was aimed at creating more competition also added to AT&T's regulatory burden.

Our attempts to turn the attention of the public to the far-reaching implications of these changes got nowhere. The reaction seemed to be: "Telephone service is fine. The rates are OK. A little competition can't hurt."

But whether or not the public was concerned about telecommunications matters, the Department of Justice certainly was. In November 1974, it filed what may have been the most massive antitrust case in history, seeking in the name of competition nothing less than the total dismemberment of the Bell System.

In 1976, while the case was still in its preliminary stages, AT&T and the independent telephone companies turned to Congress, seeking a restatement of national communications policy that would decide whether and where competition would be in the public interest. From then on, efforts to update the Communications Act of 1934 became a regular item on the congressional agenda, but the annual drive to reach a legislative consensus consistently failed to reach its goal.

Throughout this period, technology continued to advance. This new technology, much of it originating at our own Bell Laboratories, was, as I indicated earlier, inexorably wiping away the distinction between communications and data processing. Technically, the difference between the two mattered little. It was significant only because of a 1956 Consent Decree, which confined the Bell System to regulated telecommunications markets. Communications services that might be construed as data processing were accordingly out of bounds for AT&T, even though data processing companies could, at will, enter the telecommunications business. And the portion of the business they targeted. was the fastest growing and most promising.

Thus, in 1979, when I became chief executive of AT&T, the company's pressing challenge was to make its way out of the quagmire of issues in which it was trapped—legal, regulatory and legislative. But as it turned out, reaching a consensus among the key players—Congress, the Justice Department, the FCC—proved almost hopeless.

All the while, the antitrust suit formed a backdrop for the legislative and regulatory maneuvering. At one point, the

Justice Department said it would withdraw the case if Congress enacted suitable legislation. Conversely, some legislators said Congress should not act until the suit was resolved. AT&T found itself caught in the middle of a three-ring circus, and there was no ringmaster in sight.

Despite the confusion, certain realities were clear. First, regardless of specific approaches that might come out of Congress, the FCC or the courtroom, the marketplace was becoming the key instrument for governing the telecommunications industry. Second, the Bell System was perceived as too big, too powerful, too pervasive. More, not fewer, restrictions were likely. Third, time was against us. Unless the issues were resolved quickly, the market opportunities created by our own technology would pass us by. The implications of these realities were unmistakable: the Bell System would have to agree to some sort of structural change—most likely a radical restructuring.

Given the circumstances, we concluded that the antitrust issues needed to be resolved first, but not by continued litigation. That would drag on for years before a final decision could be reached, most likely in the Supreme Court. Nor would an elaborate injunctive decree be acceptable, since it would no doubt contain all of the restrictions being considered by Congress, and then some.

The only other option was to consider the divestiture solution that the Justice Department had developed—a drastic step, to be sure, but not as shattering as the remedy sought by the Justice Department when it filed the suit in 1974.

The proposal made by the Justice Department at the end of 1981 was based on the theory that the Bell System's relatively noncompetitive operations (local exchange service) ought to be separated from its competitive businesses, such as long distance service, customer premises equipment and manufacturing. While I believed divestiture was far too drastic a solution to the public-policy problems that competition posed, it finally emerged as the best among a number of unappealing alternatives.

It represented a coherent solution that promised to cut through the hopeless tangle of issues in which AT&T and the telecommunications industry were enmeshed. It would get AT&T and the local operating companies out of the courtroom and let them concentrate on running their businesses. Moreover, I was certain that divestiture could be made to work for AT&T, for the companies to be divested, for our customers, shareowners and employees, and for the nation at large. How well it can be made to work and at what cost remains to be seen, although Bell System people are determined to make the best of the situation.

Thus we accepted the government's divestiture proposal.

RESHAPING THE WORLD'S LARGEST CORPORATION

The Consent Decree established broad, basic guidelines for divestiture and called for AT&T to submit a detailed plan of reorganization to carry out its provisions. The plan would be subject to review by the Justice Department and by Judge Harold Greene of the Federal District Court in Washington.

The planning process got under way immediately. The Bell System people involved found themselves in an ironic position; they were being asked to bring to this unwanted task the same dedication, creativity and energy that they had relied on to help build the Bell System. Nonetheless, they threw themselves with vigor into what would be the largest corporate reorganization in history, dividing up a going operation that had a million employees and $150 billion in assets, that dispatched 100,000 technicians a day on service calls, and whose "operators" had daily contacts with literally millions of Americans.

Before the reorganization planning could begin in earnest, key policy issues had to be resolved. To address these issues, we formed six top-level task forces, each composed of AT&T officers and presidents of the local Bell operating companies. The composition of these task forces clearly signaled that the companies to be divested, no less than AT&T, would make the decisions affecting their futures.

The first matter to be resolved was the organization of the companies to be divested, since no other aspect of planning could get very far until a decision was made on structure. Theoretically, we had a variety of options. AT&T could spin the telephone companies off as individual entities. Or in groups. Or in one huge nationwide organization.

As in every aspect of divestiture, we based our decision on what we thought would be best for our customers, shareowners and employees. In addition, AT&T specifically pledged itself to launching the Bell operating companies in sound financial condition.

The idea of spinning the companies off as individual entities was never seriously considered. As a practical matter, it would have been difficult if not impossible to devise a way of distributing the equity of 22 separate companies among AT&T's 3.2 million shareowners that would have been practical for the companies and the shareowners. What's more, spinning off the companies separately would diminish the financial and operational strengths that go with size.

Nor did we ever contemplate divesting the companies grouped as part of a single entity, even though there was nothing in the decree to preclude this approach. We believed, however, that such a large organization would likely run into antitrust problems almost immediately, since it would have controlled two-thirds to three-quarters of the assets of the old Bell System and would have a work force of more than 600,000 people. We were keenly aware, after all, that in the final analysis, it was surely the Bell System's size and supposed power that prompted the government to seek breaking it up.

In a matter of several weeks, the task force concluded that grouping the telephone companies into regional organizations made the most sense, from the viewpoint of finances, operations and public policy. The plan that we adopted and the court later approved established the framework for the organization of the Bell operating companies as they exist today.

The arrangement was simple, clear-cut and easily understandable. At divestiture, each of the 22 telephone companies would be grouped in one or the other of seven new regional companies. All seven companies would be established so as to be roughly comparable in size and assets, large enough to maintain investor interest and support, yet small enough not to be considered unduly powerful. Each of the 22 telephone companies would retain its individual identity and serve the same areas after divestiture as before.

Such an approach, we hoped, would, to the greatest extent possible, minimize the impact of divestiture. The majority of telephone company employees could continue in the same jobs working for the same company for basic local service.

THE NEW AT&T

Once the issue of structure was decided, the other task forces began in earnest to address the remaining key issues. For example, physical assets had to be divided among AT&T and the 22 Bell operating companies. These assets included 33,000 buildings with more than 330 million square feet of space, millions of miles of cable and wire, motor vehicles, and other work equipment, materials and supplies. Similarly, rules had to be established for the assignment of personnel to either AT&T or a Bell operating company.

In a matter of months, virtually all of the conceptual planning for divestiture was completed, and the Plan of Reorganization—a document printed in book form that ran 471 pages—was filed with the court on December 16, 1982. Though some changes were later required by the court, the plan as filed served as the blueprint for divestiture, and thus represented an enormous managerial accomplishment.

Meanwhile, as literally thousands of managers and employees spent 1982 and 1983 figuring out how to dismantle the Bell System, AT&T also set about planning how to organize its own operations once January 1, 1984, arrived. The designated chief executive officers of the seven regional companies began a comparable effort for their new companies.

Broadly speaking, AT&T was organized prior to divestiture on a functional basis, even though there had been some movement during the '70s toward a market-oriented structure. Thus on the eve of divestiture the company had six main components:

1. The Bell operating telephone companies, providing basic local service, including long distance service within the states where they operated
2. AT&T Long Lines, operating the interstate and international long distance networks

3. Western Electric, which manufactured telecommunications equipment, primarily for the Bell telephone companies
4. Bell Telephone Laboratories, which conducted research and development
5. AT&T Information Systems (known for a time as American Bell, Inc.), a fully separated subsidiary, which went into operation on January 1, 1983, under new federal regulations unrelated to divestiture. It supplies customers with premises equipment (telephone, switchboards, office communications systems) and enhanced communications systems, such as certain types of data communications
6. AT&T, the parent company, consisting of "general" departments that handled staff support for the local operating companies and headquarters functions such as legal and treasury

Divestiture would, overnight, make this organizational arrangement obsolete. Even as AT&T was losing three-quarters of its assets and nearly two-thirds of its employees, it was facing intensifying competition in every aspect of its business—stiff, dogged competition: long distance; home telephones; office communications systems for business, industry and government; and switching and transmission equipment for local telephone companies.

And the competitors weren't small-fry newcomers. Their ranks included some of the world's largest corporations, foreign and domestic, possessing know-how, technology, financial resources, solid reputations. The long distance competitors were enjoying a government-mandated discount for use of the local telephone companies' plants and were thus able to undercut AT&T's prices.

The implications were clear. AT&T would have to move faster than ever before in getting products from the laboratory to the customers' homes or offices, in meeting changes in the marketplace, in responding to the wants of individual customers. In turn, these requirements dictated that we align AT&T's structure, not by function to serve the needs of our local telephone companies, but by market, to meet customer needs.

Consequently, after careful deliberation, we structured all of our organizations according to their lines of business—that is, by market, not function. And we gave chief officers of each line of business control over virtually everything affecting their operations: product strategies, development priorities, marketing and, in most cases, manufacturing. To the extent feasible and desirable, then, each line of business is vertically integrated. Such an approach means that the managers who best know the market are also the ones making key decisions about serving it from beginning to end, and have the flexibility to move swiftly when necessary, free of bureaucratic roadblocks.

The lines of business are grouped into two large sectors: AT&T Communications, providing interexchange and international telecommunications services; and AT&T Technologies, encompassing Bell Laboratories, our manufacturing units and the other parts of the company which are substantially free of regulations.

A corporate headquarters organization establishes overall policy and strategy, monitors performance and administers the general affairs of the company. The headquarters unit is relatively small, less than a tenth of the size of the headquarters staff that was necessary when AT&T owned the local Bell telephone companies.

Units within the AT&T Technologies sector are responsible for development, manufacture and marketing of network systems, business communications systems, consumer products and technology systems, such as components and electronic systems and computer systems. In foreign countries, AT&T International, a unit within the Technologies sector, develops and coordinates plans to market these products and systems.

Organizationally, we have kept Bell Laboratories within AT&T Technologies, and its chief executive continues to be responsible for directing the efforts of our technical community. We have, however, aligned development work in Bell Labs with our new business units so as to ensure a sharp focus on customer needs. Bell Laboratories has played a key role in AT&T's success. Since its founding in 1925, the Labs has averaged nearly a patent a day—more than 20,000 to date. Since AT&T's future depends so heavily on access to the latest technology, the company is firmly committed to maintaining Bell Labs' position as one of the world's preeminent industrial research and development organizations.

Despite the market orientation of the new AT&T, it would be a mistake to think that the company is merely an aggregation of loosely related subsidiaries operating autonomously as parts of a larger holding company. On the contrary, we are managing AT&T as a single enterprise. While each line of business and each sector has the freedom to run its own affairs, we set basic policy and strategic direction for the corporation as a whole, and we employ centralized accounting principles, control of cash and allocation of resources.

Thus, the new AT&T is a simple enterprise. Its current organization structure—sectors, lines of business, corporate headquarters and miscellaneous subsidiaries—is intended to provide flexibility, responsiveness, accountability and market focus.

This approach requires our managers to optimize their individual parts of the business even as they fit into the overall corporate mold—a difficult challenge, to be sure. But in the end, when a decision must be made between conflicting approaches, it will be determined by answering the question, What is the best course of action in terms of the strategies and goals of the overall enterprise?

Apart from organization structure, we made a number of moves in the months before and after divestiture that clearly showed there was indeed a new AT&T on the scene. For example, we became much more visible in countries overseas, returning to markets from which we had voluntarily withdrawn a half-century ago in order to concentrate on our domestic business. Through AT&T International, we set up offices in key cities around the globe, from London to Tokyo.

More significant, we entered into partnerships, joint ventures and other arrangements with major overseas companies so as to combine their strengths with ours. With Philips of the Netherlands we formed a joint venture, AT&T Philips, to manufacture and market switching and transmission systems in Europe and other parts of the world.

In Italy, we purchased a 25 percent interest in Olivetti, with which we began focusing on the sale of business and computer systems in the growing European market. We also agreed to sell Olivetti products in the United States—notably the company's personal computer.

In the emerging Asian market, we entered into a joint venture with Taiwan's Telecommunications Administration to manufacture and market digital switching systems. Through another joint venture, in the Republic of Korea, AT&T holds a 44 percent interest in the Gold Star Semiconductor Company, which is producing an AT&T electronic switching system.

AT&T also signed an agreement with the Spanish Industry Ministry and Spain's telecommunications authority to set up a plant that will manufacture semiconductors for the European market.

Beyond illustrating our willingness to take fresh approaches to our business, these moves underscore the fact that today the telecommunications marketplace has become worldwide. There are a number of reasons for this development, but one in particular provides the driving force: research and development of telecommunications systems and equipment has become so staggeringly expensive that an individual company cannot expect to recover its costs by selling only in its own domestic market. This fact of life also explains why foreign telecommunications manufacturers have become a significant force in the domestic market in the United States. AT&T hopes to return the favor in *their* markets.

Less than three months after divestiture, AT&T furnished another striking symbol of its emergence as a new company. We entered the general-purpose computer business with the broadest initial product line in the history of the industry—the 3B family of computers. All the 3Bs run on AT&T's popular UNIX software operating system.

From AT&T's point of view, the move into the general-purpose computer business was logical, since we had in fact been producing and selling computers for two full decades—but only for use within the Bell System. Now, with the elimination of restraints on the businesses we may pursue, we are free to apply our expertise and experience to our customers' need for total information management.

By combining our strengths in both communications and computer hardware and software, we thus can provide the nation's businesses with automation systems that are able to integrate voice, data, office, building, factory and network management. Moreover, because they were initially developed to meet the exacting requirements of our own business, where reliability and performance are absolutely essential, our computers established a new standard of performance—a downtime objective of only two minutes a year. Such reliability is becoming increasingly important to businesses as automation makes more workers and operations dependent on functioning computers.

As with all our operations and other initiatives, our steps in the international marketplace and our full-scale entry into the computer business reflect the strengths that AT&T brings into its second century: advanced technology, much of it originating at Bell Laboratories; experience in the worlds of both communications and computers; financial stability; management know-how; a work force of dedicated, skilled, loyal employees; a tradition of service and of high standards; and a commitment to satisfying our customers—on their terms, not ours.

WHAT'S AHEAD?

Because of AT&T's experience in communications, in technology, in systems management, I am confident it can play a significant role in leading the way into the Information Age, helping to bring its benefits to the economy overall and to individual Americans. It has become clear that advances in telecommunications technology—and the new products and services which they make possible—can have a widespread effect on the economy and on people's daily lives.

Because of the merger of communications and data processing, telecommunications has already become an integral part of this nation's economic infrastructure, much more so than when telecommunications usually meant communication by voice. Virtually every field of endeavor—manufacturing, health care, retailing, banking, investment, publishing, transportation—has made telecommunications an integral part of daily operations as never before. Applications of the new technology have helped improve productivity, spur innovation, cut costs and create new business opportunities.

Average Americans, if they reflect on the subject, will realize that numerous services and conveniences have already been made possible by the confluence of computer and telecommunications technology. In recent years there have come on the scene a wide range of innovations that are now considered commonplace, but which were unheard of not that long ago.

Automated bank teller machines are a good example. When today's college students were children, such machines were virtually nonexistent. Now they are almost ubiquitous, enabling people to conduct financial transactions not just between 9 A.M. and 3 P.M., Monday through Friday, but rather 24 hours a day, seven days a week. This convenience is made possible, of course, by telecommunications networks that link remote teller machines with a bank's central computer.

In the last decade, the same technology has made possible computerized state lottery systems. It has given rise to ticket-sale networks that make it possible to obtain, from among many widely scattered outlets, tickets for theater and sporting events. The technology has permitted the establishment of credit-card transactions that are fast and convenient. The list of examples can go on and on.

Thus, when we speak about new Information Age products and services, we have in mind down-to-earth, practical applications, not the far-off dreams of science-fiction writers.

For the future, there is much more to come. Scientists and engineers at AT&T Bell Laboratories and other industrial, university and government research facilities have taken vast strides in recent years in the three basic technologies that underlie the Information Age: microelectronics, photonics (or fiber optics) and software.

In the case of microelectronics, the developments are coming at a furious pace. For example, the number of components, such as transistors, that can be placed on a silicon chip has doubled every 12 to 18 months in recent years. The day of the million-component chip is at hand, and by the year 2000 it is likely that the number of components on a chip will be in the tens of millions.

Advances in fast, accurate, high-capacity fiber optics

transmission are coming at an equally rapid rate. There have already been experiments at AT&T Bell Laboratories in which 420 million bits of information per second have been transmitted error free over 125 miles without amplification. At that rate, the 30-volume Encyclopaedia Britannica can be transmitted in a few seconds. But by the time you read this, that record may well have been broken. As a result of its increasing ability, lightwave technology is assuming more and more transmission tasks in the telecommunications network.

Meanwhile, we can hope to see significant gains in the ability to produce the software necessary to guide the operation of Information Age systems so they can be tailored to specific needs and be made easy and convenient to use. To increase the productivity of programmers in the creation of software, it is likely that there will be increasing reliance on computer aids, which eventually may lead to the automatic generation of applications software.

From the technological developments that are now under way, I think it is safe to predict there will be a continuing array of innovations that will help improve the efficiency and competitive position of American business and industry and make daily life more convenient for everyone.

As their cost continues to plummet, microcomputers will be found everywhere—in cars, appliances, toys, games, cameras. Personal computers will continue proliferating, as they become easier to use and less expensive to obtain. Increasingly the computers and microcomputers found in the home will be interconnected by the telecommunications network so that, for example, remote control of appliances and heating or cooling systems will be commonplace.

The growing capacity of lightwave systems will likely make video communications and graphic data bases as widespread as ordinary telephone service. The same technology may make it possible to carry high-speed data for processing by intelligent machines. From the vast volumes of data, they could select and store whatever is of interest to a given individual—news stories about his or her hometown or selected stocks or even entertainment programs.

The growing intelligence of the telecommunications network also makes it likely that people will be able to tailor their service to their particular needs at a given moment, for example, to signal that they will accept calls only from certain telephone numbers. Moreover, it is conceivable that telephone numbers will be assignable to individuals rather than telephones. By informing a central computer of their whereabouts, people could thus have their incoming calls follow them wherever they go.

As Information Age technology evolves, new uses will probably be found for it that we cannot even imagine, just as today's telecommunications system is performing tasks that the pioneers in my business could never have dreamed of.

The driving goal of AT&T for the first 100 years of its history was to universalize telephone service, to make the telephone available to virtually everyone in America—a goal we achieved in the two decades following World War II. In the new era, our challenge will be to help universalize the Information Age, to play a leading role in harnessing its technology so as to benefit businesses and consumers across the nation and around the globe. This is a broad, challenging and imaginative goal, but one for which our experience makes us uniquely qualified. And we have already begun moving toward it with vigor.

One final word. Past generations of AT&T people gained satisfaction in building an enterprise of which they were justly proud. It was marked by high standards, by dedication, integrity, excellence and continuing achievement. Change as we have in recent years, and change as we will in the years ahead, I am determined that AT&T continue to be managed according to those standards. I want future generations of AT&T people to feel as their colleagues have over the last 100 years, that they are part of something great.

Edward R. Telling

Edward R. Telling is the tenth chairman in the 99-year history of Sears, Roebuck and Company.

Under Mr. Telling's leadership, the company has moved broadly into financial services. In 1981, Sears acquired Coldwell, Banker & Company and Dean Witter Reynolds Organization, and launched the Sears U.S. Government Money Market Trust. In 1982, Mr. Telling announced formation of Sears World Trade, Inc.

Mr. Telling began his career with Sears in 1946 as a trainee in his native Danville, Illinois. In 1948, he was named assistant manager of the Sears store in Decatur, Illinois, and later became manager of the Danville store. After serving as manager of Sears Midwestern Zone, he was named general manager of Sears retail stores in the New York metropolitan area in 1965. In 1968, he became administrative assistant to the vice-president of the eastern territory.

Mr. Telling was elected vice-president, eastern territory, and a director in 1969. He was named vice-president, Midwestern territory, in November 1974, and was elected executive vice-president, Midwest, in May 1975.

In 1976, he was elected senior executive vice-president—field, and was named chairman and chief executive officer on February 1, 1978. In a corporate restructuring program, he also served as president from January 1981 until March 1981. Mr. Telling again resumed the presidency in February 1984 and served until August 1984.

A graduate of Illinois Wesleyan University, Mr. Telling received an honorary doctor of laws degree from that institution in 1978. Mr. Telling is chairman of the trustees of the Savings and Profit Sharing Fund of Sears Employees. A director of Cox Communications, Inc., Dart & Kraft Inc., Illinois Tool Works Inc., and Dean Witter Intercapital Funds, he is also a member of the Business Council, The Business Roundtable, Northwestern University Associates, the Advisory Council of the J. L. Kellogg Graduate School of Management at Northwestern University and the Citizens Board of the University of Chicago. He is a member of the Commercial Club of the Chicago Civic Committee and a director of the Economic Club of Chicago.

4
RESTRUCTURING
FOR GROWTH

By Edward R. Telling
Chairman and Chief Executive Officer
Sears, Roebuck and Company

The job of chief executive officer can be a lonely one. Only those who have sat in the chair can appreciate what it is like to realize that they are responsible for the well-being of so many people—employees, shareholders, retirees and customers. When things go wrong a chief executive is even more alone. The job brings with it responsibilities that in good conscience can never be shared. Ultimately, only one person can make the hard choices that may determine the company's destiny.

In 1978, when I became chairman of Sears, Roebuck and Company, it was obvious to everyone that major changes were necessary, some of which would be neither pleasant nor popular. The company had become too ingrown, too set in its ways. If Sears was to regain its competitive momentum and bolster its position for the future, it had to start at the top.

A NEW COMPETITIVE ENVIRONMENT

The '70s were years of turmoil for the American economy. Various trends were emerging, each spelling trouble for Sears. Retailing was becoming a mature industry with an increasing number and variety of competitors. The rapid expansion of shopping centers was drawing to a close. Consumers were spending an increasing proportion of their incomes on services and less on goods, particularly durable goods which make up a large part of our business. Inflation was having a profound impact on the finances of Sears' customers, making home ownership more difficult and cutting into purchases of auto-related products. In many respects, Sears had been slow to respond to these shifts in society and the marketplace.

Sears' problems were evident in the slowdown of earnings growth and the uncertainty of its merchandising strategy. During the mid-1970s there were wild swings in direction. First Sears upgraded its merchandise and gave new emphasis to soft lines. This helped raise margins but allowed discounters to take market share. When Sears responded with deep price cuts, sales boomed but profits eroded. The result of these merchandising shifts was poor earnings, escalating expenses and confused customers. Financial analysts and the business press alike openly wondered whether the company had lost its will and direction. A cover story in one business magazine described the situation as "Sears, Identity Crisis."

Clearly the outlook was not favorable. If Sears were to survive—much less grow—we had to move fast. The time had come to revitalize our merchandising base, improve our profitability and move Sears into new growth areas that would take advantage of its traditional strengths.

Convinced that Sears was headed for a period of even more rapid change, it was important that everyone understand where we were headed and why. I worked that way as a store manager, a group manager and as a territorial executive vice-president. My management philosophy has always been simple: give people the jobs and the authority and then allow them the freedom to perform.

It was also important that everyone recognize that the basic values of the company would never change. Sears' efforts to steer a new course would be in line with its tradition as a merchandising leader with a trusted reputation for service to its customers. No matter what new ventures were undertaken, the company would never lose sight of its customer franchise. Merchandising would remain the cornerstone of the corporation. The challenge was to find new ways to serve Sears' huge customer base.

CHANGING THE STRUCTURE

Clearly, the first task was to unite a very fragmented organization behind a single direction. For too long Sears' retailing operations had been divided into five virtually autonomous territories, each headed by an executive vice-president who also served on the board of directors.

The telephone directory in all Sears locations mirrored this balkanization of the company. It contained a blue flyleaf which listed the territorial executive vice-president and his staff almost as if each were a king in his own kingdom, accountable to no one but himself. That philosophy of decentralization worked during the years of explosive retail growth immediately following World War II. However, with each passing year this structure became more a hindrance than a help.

By the '70s Sears was, in effect, five different merchandising companies. There was duplication of effort and a serious absence of coordination between headquarters and field. The stores looked different; they carried different lines of goods and promoted them in different ways. In an age of national television advertising, Sears was beginning to lose impact as a national retailer.

What's more, this outmoded structure failed to take advantage of the many technological advances that now made it possible to manage a huge organization from one central location. Computers, satellite communications and jet planes had shrunk the vastness of the country, yet Sears' corporate structure failed to reflect any of these cost-effective, time-saving innovations.

The fragmentation of the company was also evident in the widening split between the buying organization and the store network. I spent my whole career operating retail stores. Others rose through the buying ranks. Seldom was there any crossover. Most executives lived within the narrow confines of their side of the business. This often led to mistrust and conflict. The worst part was that there was no place to resolve these internal conflicts except in the office of the Sears chairman.

To address this situation, my predecessor hired McKinsey and Company, the management consultants, to take a hard look at Sears' corporate structure. The McKinsey people discovered that the Sears chairman had 22 separate people reporting to him. That meant he had to spend much of his time reconciling differences among the various parts of the company. Attending to these day-to-day details of the merchandising business left little time to oversee the corporation as a whole—much less plan for future growth.

The McKinsey study recommended a partial solution—establishment of an Office of the Chairman. The structure was comprised of four key executives: the chairman, the president and two new senior executive vice-president positions. I was chosen to head up the field organization, i.e., the stores, and James Button was given the buying group. This was the first attempt to unify the merchandising business and make what had become a huge, far-flung operation work as one. It was also viewed as a way to free the Sears chairman from some of the burden of daily line management.

When I became chairman in 1978 it was clear that the structure needed more substantive modification. We dissolved the Office of the Chairman in 1980 and set up a separate Merchandise Group headed by one chief executive officer. It would be up to him to complete the job of forging the buying and selling organizations into a single entity. This freed me as the new Sears corporate chairman to devote my time and energies to repositioning the corporation as a whole for the future. Sears, Roebuck and Company was now a true holding company with three equal, autonomous operating groups—Sears Merchandise Group, Allstate Insurance, and Seraco, recently formed to manage our commercial real estate and savings and loan operations.

Another key structural change involved the composition of the board of directors. Since diversification would bring us into new areas and might even involve major acquisitions down the road, it was apparent that the board could be greatly strengthened by introducing more outside directors. This was easier said than done. Traditionally, the Sears board had been dominated by retail company executives. That meant that except for the chairman of Allstate, the board represented the interests and concerns of only one segment of Sears' business. It was my contention that the new Sears holding company board must correspond to new corporate goals and direction. I was confident that all Sears' businesses would benefit from the experience, expertise and credibility additional outside directors would bring.

Beyond infusing new leadership into the board of directors, we were determined to get more young, energetic minds into key management positions, otherwise any attempt to rejuvenate Sears would be hampered by too much tradition and tired ways of thinking. Sears had many talented younger people at lower levels. The problem was they couldn't move through the management pipeline fast enough.

When it comes to the subject of management succession, I hold some very strong views. After 38 years I have come to believe that there is a limit to the contribution most senior people can make. If they have not made that contribution after six or seven years in a job, they are not likely to do so. On the other hand, if they have been effective, then they have already given their best effort. This is especially true for chief executives. It takes about three years to get a program in place and another three years to see it run and show results. After that, it is time to bring in fresh minds to keep the company vital.

Because this regenerative process was not occurring satisfactorily at Sears, we had to do something dramatic but do it in such a way that it did not hurt the people involved or hamper the company's progress. Our solution was a very attractive voluntary early retirement program from which everyone benefited.

Rarely does a chief executive come up with something that is universally applauded. The early retirement program was one of those exceptions. Almost overnight the average age of Sears' officers dropped from nearly 60 to 48. What's more, we were able to eliminate a number of redundant management positions, turning what had been a top-heavy executive structure into a leaner, more youthful organization. Morale improved immediately, because those who stayed were tremendously excited about the new opportunities for advancement. It's hard to describe what a difference this made to the vitality of the corporation.

A good example was our choice for the first chairman and chief executive officer of the new Sears Merchandise Group, Edward Brennan, 46. I knew him well and was familiar with his accomplishments, first as the group manager in Buffalo, followed by Boston, and then as executive vice-president of the southern territory. Although considerably younger than other Sears officers, I was confident that Brennan had the qualities it would take to turn the merchandising company around. More important, we shared a common view of what had to be done to reenergize the retail operations and return them to healthy profitability.

Another opportunity to inject younger blood into senior management came with the appointment of 34-year-old Phillip Purcell as Sears' first vice-president of corporate planning. As director of McKinsey and Company's Chicago office, Purcell had headed up the two-year study of Sears. He was very familiar with the corporation—the problems as well as the opportunities.

Although it is often difficult to bring outsiders into companies with strong traditions of promotion from within, Purcell was already perceived and accepted by many in the organization as uniquely qualified for this new position. Not only did he bring a fresh point of view but he had the formal strategic and operational planning skills most of us lacked. His input would be critical for the tough job that lay ahead.

THE PLANNING PROCESS

One of my main goals as chairman was to create a mechanism that would enable us to agree on a set of objectives and allocate the resources of the corporation accordingly. My role as chairman would be to monitor the results in view of our stated goals.

I do not believe a chief executive can or should ever delegate final responsibility. However, he can delegate a great deal of authority and let everyone know it. Then each individual is free to do his work and enjoy the great feeling of accomplishment that comes with doing it well.

The best leaders that I have known over the years accomplished their goals without making people feel that they were being led. The discipline behind this technique is a strong planning process.

As we began to unify our merchandising operations under a

single authority, we encountered resistance. While it made good business sense to have national planning, standards and promotion for all our stores, it was a struggle to bring them about.

Perhaps the most traumatic change of all was abolition of a bookkeeping system referred to as the "overbilling account." It was started many years ago by the Sears buying organization to help finance new machinery for our suppliers. Gradually, the overbilling account evolved into a huge fund totaling hundreds of millions of dollars which was then used to finance national promotions including the markdown of goods.

Sears buyers would sell goods to the stores at prices well above cost and then use the differential for product development and promotional expenses. The store managers, in turn, would mark up the goods according to their own sales and profit system. As a result, by the late '70s, Sears had become seriously overpriced and noncompetitive.

To make matters worse, this discretionary fund distorted our whole merchandising effort and made company-wide planning virtually impossible. Because overbilling was also built into the compensation system, senior management had little incentive to fight the status quo. It had become part of the company culture and was dangerously skewing all our efforts.

That's why we had to replace overbilling with a planning process that would define at the beginning of the year realistic projections of a department's sales, gross profit and market share. We then could determine what resources would go into advertising, promotion and so on. Today, I don't believe anyone would want to reinstate the overbilling system, but because it had become a kind of cushion that allowed people to obscure mistakes in judgment, its demise took some time for the organization to accomplish and to accept.

THE MOVE TO DIVERSIFY

At the same time fundamental changes were being made in Sears' basic merchandising business, a drive toward diversification was launched. Obviously any major action would have to be endorsed by the Sears board of directors, but there would also have to be broad approval at all levels of the organization. For that reason we formed a strategic planning committee comprised of senior management from Sears merchandising, insurance and real estate operations.

Not only did this committee open lines of communication between the separate parts of the corporation, but it also provided the necessary forum in which conflicting views could be productively aired, explored and resolved in a way that would move Sears foward.

At the outset there was little agreement about Sears' future direction. Many people within the company believed that Sears should maintain its traditional role as a retailer and not risk pursuing major new businesses. Some favored diversification and championed activities that involved advanced electronics, telecommunications and their applications in the home. Others proposed that the company become heavily involved in home entertainment. In the late '70s both cable television and direct broadcast satellites appeared to be attractive growth opportunities.

I personally favored expanded participation in consumer financial services. However, I did not want to risk overlooking any options. To be effective I knew the final diversification strategy must come from a consensus of the officers on the committee after careful evaluation of all the alternatives. It was important that all senior management share a real sense of ownership in any plan that was adopted.

The process began with an exhaustive study of American business, examining entire industries as well as leading participants on the basis of current profitability and the potential for growth. In particular, we sought situations where Sears could bring something to the party, where our reputation, marketing know-how and financial muscle would come into play.

Given the size and nature of our core merchandising and insurance businesses, we confined our studies to major industries and even then we only considered those businesses in which Sears already had, or had the means to become, a major factor in a relatively short time. That meant that any new business had to have a large revenue potential with excellent returns.

In addition, we established several other guidelines. The

new business had to be consumer-oriented, because Sears is fundamentally a merchandising company. It had to be a business where Sears' image of trust could make a competitive difference. It also had to be a business that was national in scope and would take advantage of Sears' more than 800 retail stores coast to coast. Finally, it had to be a business that would allow us to provide greater value to our customers. Sears would never diversify for purely financial reasons. We were only interested in partnerships from which all involved could benefit.

THE FINANCIAL SERVICES FIT

Consumer financial services met all the criteria. In fact, it was a natural outgrowth of what we had been doing for decades. For example, since 1911, Sears had offered its customers credit at a time when most banks refused to make similar consumer loans without collateral. Today, more than half of Sears' merchandise sales are made on credit. We have about 26 million active credit card accounts, with total credit receivables averaging more than $11 billion annually. Thus our credit activities have become a significant part of our business.

In the insurance field we were already an important institution. Allstate was the nation's second largest property/liability insurer and also ranked in the top 1 percent of America's legal reserve life insurance companies. More important, Allstate, following its own path of diversification, had already entered the mortgage insurance and mortgage packaging businesses through its acquisition of San Francisco-based PMI in the mid-1970s. Through Allstate, we also owned the Sears Savings Bank, the 25th largest thrift institution in the country.

Taking these factors into account, it was apparent that Sears already had many of the attributes of a broad-based consumer financial services organization. Nor were we the only ones to reach this conclusion. As early as 1974, Citicorp Chairman Walter Wriston had described Sears as potentially "the biggest bank in the country." Peter Drucker agreed. In his book, *Managing in Turbulent Times*, Drucker predicted that consumer banking would become a separate industry from traditional banking, and that "Sears could be a national chain focused on the needs of the American family."

My own view was that many of Sears' 40 million customers were not being well served either by the banks or by the securities industry. On the one hand, banks operating in a highly regulated environment had never had to be sensitive to the needs of consumers. As for stockbrokers, they historically catered to the wealthy. Because Sears had built its reputation on serving the merchandising and insurance needs of the American middle class, it was logical to conclude that given the right combination of products and services we had a unique opportunity to develop a new kind of broad-based consumer financial services institution.

The next step was to identify the missing pieces that would make us a fully diversified provider of financial services. We knew that if we chose that field, we would want to be involved in the key activities in consumers' financial lives. This would mean participating in consumer banking—deposit-taking and lending—personal insurance, residential real estate and personal investments. These were the major links in the emerging financial services industry. They were also the springboards to launch other profitable financial services businesses such as mortgage insurance and national relocation management.

Next, we set out to assess realistically our competence in these different areas. For example, through Allstate we were strong in insurance and had a good foundation in consumer banking, but interstate banking laws restricted our savings and loan activities to California. On the other hand, we had no presence whatsoever in securities or residential real estate brokerage, although Sears, through a subsidiary called Homart, had been a major shopping center developer since 1959.

The decision now was how best to proceed—either build from within or acquire. Traditionally, Sears has built new businesses from the ground up. Allstate is a prime example. Homart is another. However, in this case, that approach made little sense. Competitive and deregulatory pressures were forcing rapid consolidation in the industry. Two of the largest securities firms had already been acquired by financial service conglomorates. Others were sure to follow. If Sears were to establish a national foothold in either field, we had to act quickly before the window closed.

In May 1981 a special meeting of the board of directors was called. We wanted them to understand the evolution and direction of our thinking in some detail so we organized a series of presentations.

First, the heads of our three business groups—Sears Merchandise Group, Allstate and Seraco, our commercial real estate division—outlined their prospects and plans for the next five and 10 years respectively. Each explained where his group was headed, how much capital would be required to achieve the goals set and what kind of return on investment could realistically be expected.

Then Richard Jones, our chief financial officer, summed up the situation. He explained what the bottom line would be if Sears continued with its present business mix. And it wasn't bad. On the other hand, when we added it all up, it wasn't good enough. The best return on investment that could be achieved would not be good enough for Sears' 350,000 shareholders.

Now it was time for my presentation. I explained to the board that if we kept on doing what we were doing, even if we did it very well, it was clear that the company would not achieve a satisfactory level of growth. It was time to try some new things which would take advantage of Sears' historic strengths as well as the trends we saw in the marketplace. As a result, I recommended that we expand our presence in consumer financial services. But to position ourselves more strongly in that industry I proposed that Sears acquire a securities broker and a residential real estate company, the only two significant components lacking.

Having made the case, I asked for comments and suggestions. There was a long silence, and Donald Rumsfeld, president and chief executive officer of G.D. Searle & Co., leaned back and said, "Well, Ed, when is the press conference?" Everyone laughed. It was good to know that we had cleared that hurdle. The next step was to decide which firms to acquire.

THE RIGHT PARTNERS

Extensive market research showed how customers rated the national securities firms. We found that Dean Witter Reynolds, the fifth largest, came out on top in nine of 11 categories. That impressed us. Dean Witter also ranked second to Merrill Lynch in the number of account executives. The firm had a conservative balance sheet and a reputation for integrity and trustworthiness to match our own.

In October 1981 we announced plans to acquire Dean Witter. By coincidence that same week, we made public our intentions to acquire Coldwell Banker, the nation's largest full-service real estate brokerage firm.

The choice of Coldwell Banker was even more clear-cut. By any measure the company was the unchallenged leader in both residential and commercial real estate. In addition, Sears already held a minority position in the firm. The only reservation was that Coldwell Banker's senior management might resist becoming part of a wholly owned Sears subsidiary.

This was a major consideration. Sears had no intention of becoming embroiled in an unfriendly takeover. It was totally inconsistent with our business philosophy. Fortunately, we were able to assure the Coldwell Banker management that we wanted them to run their company in their own fashion. At the same time, we encouraged them to draw upon the Sears customer base and financial strength to make their real estate business grow even faster.

With the addition of Dean Witter and Coldwell Banker, Sears was positioned for the kind of long-term growth envisioned. However, we were realists. No one expected any instant miracles. We were prepared for a long period of base building, including major investments.

For example, while other securities firms were contracting their retail activities, Dean Witter planned to expand its force of account executives to 11,000 by 1988, twice the number the firm had when Sears acquired it. To be sure, this was an ambitious goal but not unrealistic in light of the public's increasing interest in personal investment opportunities. In addition, Sears' customer base represented a huge untapped potential for the firm's services.

We planned aggressive expansion for Coldwell Banker as well. When we acquired the firm in late 1981, it had 370 residential and commercial real estate offices. Our goal was to increase the number of offices to 3,000 by 1990. With the complete Coldwell Banker network in place, Sears' customers would then have access in one location not only to real estate brokerage services but a full array of ancillary services including mortgages, mortgage insurance and title insurance.

The Sears Financial Network with 300 in-store locations has been perhaps the most visible example of Sears' ability to offer a broad assortment of financial services to our customers in a convenient, comfortable environment, the Sears sales floor. By 1984 nearly 40 percent of all new Dean Witter accounts were opened through these in-store locations. And the potential is huge.

At the time of the acquisition, research showed that 80 percent of Sears' customers either had never had a brokerage account or did not have an active relationship with a stockbroker. Yet, more than 11 million Sears' credit card holders had annual household incomes exceeding the average income level of all U.S. stockholders. The in-store distribution channel has proved equally beneficial for Allstate, Coldwell Banker and Sears Savings Bank.

A SEARS WORLD TRADING COMPANY

If anything, Sears' diversification strategy has been fundamental and consistent. In every instance we have sought to leverage the company's traditional strengths and position it for the long term. For that reason we saw the development of a U.S.-based international trading company as yet another logical extension of Sears' consumer franchise. Again, we took our cue from trends in the marketplace.

By the '80s, global sourcing of products was increasingly becoming a way of life. No longer did manufacturers always own the producing assets. As for distribution, it was becoming more extensively value-added with such new services offered as sales information and information management. Even the shrill voices of protectionism had been unable to halt this trend toward a global economy. Here, perhaps, was another opportunity for Sears to make a unique contribution.

The idea also made sense given the unstable political and economic climate in many regions of the world. As part of our corporate restructuring we had already begun to divest many of our foreign holdings, particularly in Latin America, where uncertain conditions made it difficult for us to operate at a profit. We believed that a trading company would give Sears a new role in an expanding world economy plus allow us the investment flexibility our previous international strategy had lacked. After weighing all the factors, we formed a new subsidiary, Sears World Trade, Inc., in late 1982.

The original concept called for Sears World Trade to act as a middleman, providing such skills as product development, trade consulting services and international marketing. It was our intention to concentrate initially in consumer products, an area where we had long experience.

While we were sure of our strengths, such as a solid international network of suppliers, the ability to raise capital, and worldwide recognition of Sears' name and reputation, we also recognized some shortcomings. Sears lacked the foreign contacts, intimate knowledge of local conditions, and the marketing and distribution organization necessary to compete successfully in international marketplaces. It would take time, resources and the right management team to realize our vision. But then we knew we were looking at a long-term proposition. There were no role models upon which to pattern this enterprise. The most optimistic scenario called for Sears World Trade to make a material contribution to the corporation in five years or perhaps less.

Because we wanted Sears World Trade to be totally distinct from our merchandising company, we established the headquarters in Washington, D.C., away from Chicago. The Merchandise Group has years of history and a distinct style of management. As a new type of merchandising entity, we believed it best that Sears World Trade be allowed to develop its own mode of operations. To instill new ideas, as well as help develop international business contacts, we also encouraged the recruitment of key executives from outside the corporate family.

Unfortunately, as sometimes happens, the cart was put before the horse. The leadership at Sears World Trade lost sight of the original plan. For example, an impressive headquarters staff was assembled, yet the product and service delivery system it was to support never materialized. To make matters worse, Sears' vision of slow, steady growth and a low profile was challenged by ambitious statements from some subsidiary executives. Their forecasts unreasonably raised expectations about performance that the company could never realistically hope to meet.

There was only one thing to do—change the management at the top. As most chief executives would agree, decisions like this can be the most painful. But when something has to be done it is best to do it quickly and get it behind you. Agonizing over why people may have disappointed you will not make a bad situation better. No matter how a chief executive looks at it, the responsibility is still his.

In restrospect, Sears World Trade should have been launched quietly under the corporate umbrella. That strategy proved successful in the development of Sears Business System Centers, our chain of computer outlets. Sears' first entry into specialty retailing was deliberately guided from the corporate level through initial planning and testing. Only when it became a turnkey operation was the chain handed over to the Merchandise Group to run. The stores have performed, but it has been a quiet success with very little publicity about sales and profits.

Fortunately, the basic concept underlying Sears World Trade is sound. As is true with many new ventures, there were tactical errors in execution but not enough to make us doubt the company's long-term potential for growth. After all, it took more than 10 years of retail store expansion before Sears proved that experiment a success. With new, seasoned line management in place, we can afford to wait for Sears World Trade to mature.

THE FUTURE

From the moment I took charge of Sears, I knew that we had to extend our vision beyond the familiar terrain and look into the future. We would have to take a series of calculated risks. A chief executive must be both decisive and extremely patient, ready to grasp an opportunity when he sees it, but willing to accept the fact that major change takes time and mistakes will inevitably be made along the way. Few new endeavors succeed overnight.

The single most important concept that I have tried to instill in the organization in the seven years that I have been chairman is that management must continually seek new possibilities for growth. If a company is not moving forward it is probably falling behind, and that law of the competitive jungle has become less forgiving with each passing year. At the same time, it is important to recognize that success, while important, is not everything. The main point is to keep striving.

Toward that end, we have worked to create a climate that encourages intelligent risk-taking. Sears was built by entrepreneurs—managers who took risks even when the chances for personal gain were far from certain. Our goal has been to balance the rewards and punishments and increase the chances for personal gain. Managers must see opportunities for reward—otherwise they may stop trying. Today, we see the entrepreneurial spirit returning to the company. There is every reason to believe that spirit will continue to flourish.

In the final analysis, everything starts with people. Only people can bring new vitality to a venerable organization. If chief executives could have only one talent, most would ask for the ability to pick good people, to put them in the right jobs and then have the wisdom to stay out of their way. At the same time, you want them to know that you are there when they need you.

Sometimes you discover that you know more about the job than the person selected. But never think it is because you are so smart. It simply means that you have put the wrong person in that position. When that happens all you can do is change horses. If he can't run on the track, there is nothing to be gained from whipping him. It's time to get a new horse.

That's why I believe the most crucial part of any chief executive's job is to pick the right successor. The moment a new chairman sits down at the desk, his first thought should be how best to plan for future leadership.

I am confident that my successor knows the course and has

the speed set for the next watch. However, that does not mean that he will become a mere caretaker on the bridge. He has his own ideas—and he should. My concern in the choice of a successor is that I feel comfortable with his way of thinking. If you are looking for leadership qualities, you have to watch an individual for years, so you feel quite sure about how he will approach different situations.

You must also be certain that your choice pleases the people below you in the organization as well as those on the board of directors. You want them on your side for the right reason—because they agree with the decision.

If there is a perfect way to prepare someone to be a chief executive officer, I have missed it. A person must occupy the chair himself to understand the tremendous responsibility that is now his and his alone. The best advice one can give potential candidates is "be prepared" should you be fortunate enough to move ahead to that next job. Even then, few chief executives will ever know for sure why it was that lightning struck. In many respects, it is the same type of uncertainty each will face during his tenure at the top.

Douglas D. Danforth

Douglas Danforth, an executive with broad general management experience in this country and abroad, became chairman and chief executive officer of Westinghouse Electric Corporation on December 1, 1983. He was elected a director, vice-chairman and chief operating officer in 1978, the position he filled until being elected CEO.

Mr. Danforth began his career with Westinghouse in 1955 as executive vice-president and general manager of Industria Electrica de Mexico, an affiliate in Mexico City. Six years later, he was transferred to corporate headquarters in Pittsburgh as assistant to the vice-president of manufacturing. He was then appointed general manager of the control divisions. In 1963, he became executive in charge of the industrial group and the following year vice-president and general manager of the consumer group. Mr. Danforth later served as senior executive vice-president of the corporation's former Industry Products Company and, for five years, as executive vice-president of the components and materials group. He was elected president of Industry Products in 1974, and vice-chairman and chief operating officer in 1978.

Mr. Danforth earned a bachelor's degree in mechanical engineering from Syracuse University in 1947. In 1983, he was awarded an honorary doctor of laws degree by Bethany College in West Virginia.

Active in a number of financial, industrial, academic, civic and cultural groups, Mr. Danforth is a director of the PNC Financial Corporation (formed by the merger of Pittsburgh National Corporation and Provident National Corporation),

PPG Industries, Inc., and Whirlpool Corporation. He is a trustee of Carnegie-Mellon University, Lehigh University and Syracuse University, his alma mater. He serves as well on the board of visitors of the University of Pittsburgh Graduate School of Business. He is a trustee of the Committee for Economic Development and a member of the Business-Higher Education Forum. Mr. Danforth is also a trustee of Allegheny Health Services, Inc., and the Allegheny Trails Council-Boy Scouts of America. He is vice-chairman of the board of the River City Brass Band.

He was the 1984 general chairman of the United Way of Southwestern Pennsylvania campaign, and the chairman of the business advisory committee of the Institute for Training the Handicapped in Advanced Technology. He also served as chairman of the 1984 Negro Educational Emergency Drive.

Mr. Danforth is on the executive committee for the Allegheny Conference on Community Development and is a director of the American Productivity Center and the Pittsburgh Trust for Cultural Resources. Also, he is a member of the Policy Committee for the Business Council of Pennsylvania and a director of the United States Chamber of Commerce.

5
HANDLING CHANGE—
THE KEY TO CORPORATE
SURVIVAL

By Douglas D. Danforth
Chairman and Chief Operating Officer
Westinghouse Electric Corporation

The success of a company depends on a great many things, so I am always skeptical of those who would attribute it to a single factor. But my years in managing businesses and observing the experience of others have convinced me that the following statement is true:

To be successful now and in the years to come, a company must be able to handle change.

By "handle" I mean anticipating change as much as possible—responding promptly and intelligently to change as it occurs and initiating change when opportune.

Though it ebbs and flows, change is a continuing process. It never stops. The strategic ability to adapt to economic, social and technological change determines whether a company thrives and grows or withers and dies.

Some of the biggest stories on the financial pages during recent times concern how companies are surviving the difficult changes of the '80s—and how some are not. I find this of more than academic interest since Westinghouse is within a year of its 100th anniversary. Only 10 companies in Fortune's top 100 are that old. How did a company such as Westinghouse survive 100 years? And what will it take to keep going successfully?

Since George Westinghouse, the famous inventor and entrepreneur, started the company in 1886, the forces of change have been continuous. Yet three distinct periods of change are evident:

- 1886 through the turn of the century
- World War II and the post-war period
- 1974 to the present

Each of these periods required management to handle change with the greatest skill. Our management won some and it lost some. But the fact that the company is going strong today certainly suggests that management won more than it lost.

THE FOUNDATION

From the beginning, change and, more specifically anticipation of change and technological innovation, put the company into business. George Westinghouse may have been one of the first industrialists to recognize the importance of the systems approach. He lived at a time when industry was growing, urbanization was taking place and new inventions were coming fast. Thomas Edison's electric light bulb was only a few years old. The Electrical Age had arrived, but it had its problems. To use the direct current then available, machines and factories had to be located close to a generating station—perhaps within a mile.

Mr. Westinghouse, who was both a visionary thinker and a practical engineer, correctly saw a great business opportunity awaiting whoever could create a workable electrical system that would make electrical energy more widely applicable. His creative juices began flowing when he read a London technical journal one day in 1885. The article was an account of a new invention called a converter which would step alternating current up or down in voltage and perhaps make possible transmission of the energy over longer distances. He envisioned the changes that would result from such a system and he lost no time.

Fortunately, Mr. Westinghouse was not possessed of an

N.I.H. (not-invented-here) mentality. He acquired patent rights to the basic product—the transformer—from an Englishman named Gibbs and a Frenchman named Gaulard. He recruited the brilliant young Serbian Nikola Tesla, who already had worked out the fundamentals of the polyphase alternating current system (which is used worldwide today). And he surrounded himself with a group of bright, young engineers who developed the motor, the meter and other components needed to put the system into practical use.

He sent William Stanley to Great Barrington, Massachusetts, to set up an experimental a/c lighting system to prove it could be done. He demonstrated to the world the feasibility of the Tesla system by lighting the Columbian exposition in Chicago in 1893, even though to do it he had to invent a light bulb that would not infringe the Edison patents.

He proved the system in practical application by winning the contract to design and build the first waterwheel generators of their size and kind and harnessed the power of Niagara Falls.

Management courage, daring, willingness to take risks and promotional flair characterized this first management. There was intense opposition by big-name competitors. Leading those who opposed the new a/c technology, ostensibly on safety grounds, was none other than Thomas Edison himself who saw his direct current system threatened. Scare headlines appeared in the press, attempting to discredit the new "Westinghouse current," as it was being called. A faint-hearted management would have failed.

But the courageous and change-oriented management of George Westinghouse had one fatal weakness—lack of financial astuteness. He lost control of his company in 1908 and the bankers took over.

History has judged this early entrepreneur as having foreseen and promptly acted upon technological and social change with such skill that the Industrial Revolution was given new life and acceleration. Its horizons were enormously expanded. And in the process, the company that Westinghouse founded was thrust into the forefront of American industry.

CHANGE FOSTERED BY WAR

The second great period of change—the World War II era—happened after a relatively steady period of growth within Westinghouse. From 1908 to 1938, the management continued to capitalize on technological advances, leading to such new businesses as radio broadcasting and electrical home appliances.

Invention's mother is not always necessity. Radio originally was a plaything of a Westinghouse engineer named Frank Conrad who pursued his hobby in his garage. When spoken signals became monotonous, he began to play phonograph records — the first disk jockey.   Other amateurs then experimenting with the new toy began tuning him in and sending letters requesting him to play his records at a certain time so they could prove to their skeptical friends that music. indeed could be transmitted through the air.

In 1920, a Westinghouse vice-president correctly anticipated the potential of their actions. On November 2, 1920, the first commercial radio broadcast—the election results of the Harding-Cox presidential race—was made from atop the Westinghouse East Pittsburgh manufacturing complex. As they say, "the rest is history."

By the beginning of World War II, radio was considered an important and valuable segment of the Westinghouse portfolio. Today broadcasting and cable still comprise a significant portion of our business.

But the importance of management's ability to gauge the course of future events correctly and see change coming was never more clearly demonstrated than at the time of World War II and its aftermath.

In 1939, the chief executive of Westinghouse, Chairman A. W. Robertson, and the number two man, President George H. Bucher, believed the peacetime market was likely to disappear in the near future. They arranged a meeting at the White House with President Franklin D. Roosevelt to emphasize the desire and capabilities of their company to serve the nation in the period ahead. Although their presentation was based on the long-term commitment to research and advanced technology, they acted quickly in laying the groundwork for this market shift.

Robertson and Bucher held some interesting cards to play:

Dr. Clinton Hanna, a scientist who was experimenting in gyroscopic control of steel mill motors at the Research Laboratories, had an idea for development of a device which would stabilize the gun on an army tank so it could be fired accurately even while the tank was in motion over rough terrain.

Dr. I. F. Mourmtseff, a Russian-born scientist at the Laboratories, had been experimenting for several years on the curious behavior of shortwave radio beams. He had found that when he transmitted shortwave beams from the hilltop laboratories toward the East Pittsburgh plant a mile away, the automobiles traveling along the Lincoln Highway which ran in between the two locations interrupted the shortwave radio transmission. Radar soon was to use the same principle. It was an early Westinghouse radar set that, on the morning of December 7, 1941, enabled an army corporal to detect correctly the approach of Japanese aircraft at Pearl Harbor. Unfortunately, his warning was ignored.

Dr. Stewart Way, who had been working on gas turbines for electric power generation, had in hand the technology which would lead three years later to the first American-designed jet-aircraft engine.

And Dr. Harvey Rentschler's ability to produce the rare metal uranium in pure form for lamp research was to play a vital role in helping Enrico Fermi build the first atomic pile, or reactor, at Stagg Field in Chicago—leading to development of the atomic bomb.

Rarely had management held cards which would win such big tricks in the years ahead. But it took a farsighted management to recognize the coming changes and to play the hand in timely fashion.

The postwar period called for some of the most vital decisions on the corporate portfolio until the current day. What businesses should a corporation be in? What businesses should it drop? Is there any more important question that can face a chief executive?

With the coming of peace in 1945, our management faced difficult portfolio decisions. Many new technologies had come to the fore during the war. Radar, nuclear energy, electronics, computers and jet propulsion were among them. Westinghouse had played important roles in all, but now had to decide which to include in the peacetime portfolio.

Could we go into both computers and nuclear power? If not, which? Should the corporation attempt to be a major factor in the peacetime defense business or leave that market to those companies that devote 100 percent of their effort to defense work? We had great technical competence in the new jet propulsion technology. Should we stay in that business?

President Gwilym A. Price decided to put full effort behind the development of nuclear power and not enter the data-processing computer field. Westinghouse went on to win world leadership in nuclear power, a field which is a profitable part of our portfolio today.

And Westinghouse was to continue as a major factor in the defense business, with emphasis on radar technology. Defense today is a billion-dollar-plus business which not only provides important sales volume but also generates new technology which is useful across the broad spectrum of Westinghouse operations.

The management decision to stay with jet engine production looked good at the end of the war, but soon became a dubious one. The smaller peacetime market would not support four major U.S. jet engine manufacturers. So when Westinghouse ran into production problems with a new engine design, the business was abandoned. No doubt this was a blow to the pride of our aviation gas turbine experts, but it was a wise move for Westinghouse stockholders.

After the war, the appliance business came back strongly and for the next several decades grew vigorously. Soon Betty Furness became the nation's best-known appliance salesperson through the wonders of television. How many people could then have guessed that Westinghouse would go out of that business entirely by the mid-1970s?

The business portfolio decisions made in the postwar era were critical to the health and survival of Westinghouse. As with any other company, our portfolio decisions were the job of top management, and ultimately the CEO, and they were made when it was apparent that continuation of certain of our businesses was no longer in the best interests of the stockholders. These decisions required our chief executives to prepare businesses for divestiture, contraction or closedown. These actions produced a positive result for all parties involved.

A more recent example was the sale of our lamp business in 1983. We had been in that business more than 50 years and had never lost money. But we could see the need to put at least $50 million of new capital into it each year for the next five years. Even then it was questionable whether the investment would generate an adequate return.

It was not line management that decided to sell. The management committee made that decision. The sale freed up $200 million of assets to deploy where we could generate a greater return on the corporate investment. This was clearly in the best interests not only of our stockholders but of the vast majority of Westinghouse employees who depend on the corporation's success for their livelihood in the years ahead.

Since that sale was made to a successful company which continued the business, even our lamp employees did not suffer from the transaction, a much happier outcome than occurs in the case of most business shut downs.

I've always said, "Don't fall in love with a business. Fall in love with your people, but don't fall in love with a piece of steel or glass or plastic. Those things will come and go because of changes you can't control."

Just as it is important to know when to get out of a business, it is equally vital to know when to go into one. Responding to change means being alert to and taking timely advantage of new business opportunities.

AFTER OPEC...A NEW BALL GAME

Responding to change in the decade that followed the unforeseeable OPEC oil price hike has made Westinghouse an almost completely different company than it was in 1974. Our strategy became clearly a matter of responding as promptly and intelligently as possible as events occurred.

The two earlier periods of great change for Westinghouse—the turn of the century and World War II—had been opportunities well-taken. But this third period of great change presented a different kind of challenge.

The oil crisis completely reversed the curve of utility growth which had held since George Westinghouse's day. As the world suddenly searched for ways to conserve energy, utilities found themselves with excess capacity and the sale of electrical apparatus such as turbines and generators virtually halted.

Westinghouse, whose main business had been supplying apparatus to electric utilities and industry, was faced with change of the most substantial kind. One of its biggest markets had shrunken away.

But management responded in four ways:

- First, we supplied services to our utility customers and emphasized the service businesses throughout the company. We recognized that the entire economy was changing from one based primarily on manufacturing to one based more heavily on services.

  Westinghouse has shifted away from some businesses that depend primarily on low-cost manufacturing. Nearly half of our sales volume today comes from service-related business.

  A lot of people think that because the sale of nuclear power plants in the United States has been a dormant business for the past several years, the nuclear industry is in jeopardy. What they don't realize is that nuclear is now largely a service-type business. Except for nuclear fuel, it involves little manufacturing.

- Second, where we were manufacturing, we capitalized on advanced technology and engineering systems expertise. Our flourishing defense business is a good example.

- Third, we emphasized high-growth, high-margin businesses and acquisitions in businesses with high-margin potential, such as cable and robotics.

- And, fourth, we launched a corporate-wide program on quality and productivity.

The management responses to the changes of the '70s and '80s, have led to the near total restructuring of the company

George Westinghouse started nearly 100 years ago. He might only recognize the name on the door if he returned today.

HOW WE ARE ORGANIZED TODAY

We have 30 separate and largely autonomous business units which operate as independent companies as much as possible, because in today's economy this is the way they can best compete. This does not mean we have become a holding company or a conglomerate. All growth resources remain corporate property—capital, strategic money, R&D funding—and are controlled at the top.

Business units are grouped together under group presidents who are on the Corporate Management Committee. This takes into account the financial, technological and marketing synergism of the various business units. It also binds them together with a set of corporate ground rules that include such broad strategies as quality and productivity, portfolio direction, growth and innovation, executive development and communications.

Another change which the management of any company today has had to recognize in its organization and marketing strategies is the existence of world markets. We compete today not just with companies in New York or Illinois or California. We compete with companies in Tokyo, Seoul, Singapore, Frankfurt, London and São Paulo. We don't have the big U.S. market to ourselves anymore. Every multinational in the world sells here, which has made necessary a change in the thinking of management in every major industry. This is one main reason my company is no longer interested in businesses that depend principally on low-cost manufacturing.

To cope with changes such as the growth of the services economy and the development of world markets, Westinghouse has evolved from a strictly U.S. electrical equipment manufacturer to a diversified company serving a wide range of markets and customers throughout the world. And we are moving into many new, promising areas. Capitalizing on new business opportunities is essential for any company to gain or hold a position of leadership in today's world economy, and in the world economy of the future.

MANAGEMENT STYLE

I am a strong believer in the need for a chief executive to stay in personal touch with the key people in his organization. Everybody is dedicated to the need for delegating authority and responsibility—one man can't run a big corporation. But there is a fine line between such dedication and abdication of responsibility as the final decision-maker on major issues.

I have sometimes been accused by my colleagues of overmanaging. And it is quite right that an executive can't overmanage because it stifles the development of people. But the opposite sin is even worse. You can't delegate authority and responsibility and then just walk away. The chief executive must walk a narrow line between too much and too little managing.

Management Committees

I find the management committee a very workable arrangement. My management committee, consisting of the top seven executives in the corporation, meets at least twice a month and more often if necessary. It considers a wide range of matters—major investment decisions, important personnel changes, policy changes—and in most of these areas decision is reached by consensus. If consensus isn't reached, then it is the CEO's role to make the decision.

In our management committee meetings we attempt to make the decision then and there, rather than put it off until the next meeting. Postponing decisions is not helpful unless a very complicated matter, which obviously needs more study and data, is under consideration.

More often than not, we will reach a "go or not go" decision on the matter in one meeting. Once the meeting ends, the CEO knows the team will carry out the consensus policy in a united front even though there may have been a dissenting vote or two. There can be no fragmentation at the top, and I have never found that to be a problem.

Managing for Performance

It doesn't matter if employees are key executives or people on the shop floor, the ability to manage their activities and get the most effective performance from them is the essence of leadership.

Starting with the management team, I believe success is built on trust and trust is built on actions. For example, a chief executive has to have a high tolerance for bad news if he is to expect his managers to "give it to him straight" when things are not going right.

Don't shoot the messenger who brings bad news. The executive who loses his temper when somebody reports a failure or mistake is obviously never going to have any more mistakes reported to him. He will learn of them the hard way—too late. If people know their managers can deal with bad news or disappointment, they will address problems early on—while there is still time to take corrective action. When reports are in early enough, all of the skills and resources of the corporation can be mustered to solve the problem.

Several recent examples of this come to mind. When the economy in Brazil began to collapse, we knew we would have big problems unless we could work them out early. We reorganized and streamlined our businesses down there and, although there has been a small impact on earnings, it could have been much worse if we hadn't moved in right away.

Domestically, the synfuels business was one in which we had invested millions of dollars. Then came the winds of change. Oil prices started dropping. We were able to handle that one because our people were willing to talk about it early enough to take effective action. I think our management, and probably management generally, has become more sophisticated about the need to face up quickly to bad news and the negative impact of change.

We like this process in our company because it embraces all kinds of things—competition, environmental considerations, new technology, economic trends, trade barriers and others. And it wraps everything up in financial terms. It says: given these considerations, here are the financial expectations for this business over the next period.

Once those goals and objectives are reviewed and approved by the management committee, we expect the business unit manager to view this strategic plan as a commitment.

I'll call a manager after a meeting and ask: "Do you really feel that this objective is achievable?" If the manager says yes, I point out that I am going to be making corporate decisions based on the strategic plan and I must be sure it is realistic. Otherwise, I will be making bad decisions for the corporation.

Once in a while this personal approach will change the response of the individual business unit manager. A manager will level with me—about not really feeling confident that the objectives can be attained without some small miracles happening. In these cases, we ask managers to go back over their plans and come back again in 90 days or so with a commitment with which they feel comfortable. Of course, it can work in reverse, too. If the business unit managers come in with strategic plans that we know are "pieces of cake," we'll level with them about that. This process results in a personal commitment between me as CEO and the business unit manager. I believe the personal relationship is an important part of the process.

EMPLOYEE STABILITY

The management of a company's employees—its "human resources"—has become one of the most difficult problems in industry in recent years as automation becomes a "must" in most production processes. Robots are taking over many routine tasks that used to require the muscles, hands and fingers of industrial workers. It is not a question of choice here. The company that lags in its use of robotics and automation soon will become noncompetitive and go the way of the buggy whip manufacturers.

In the long run, the workers who are displaced by robots will find new jobs opening up in growing service areas and in new industries. But in the short run, there remain problems of temporary worker displacement, needed retraining and lack of labor mobility.

In the interim, management must use maximum skills and

ingenuity to bridge the gap. This is most important because the only way you can have an esprit de corps in an organization is for your employees to have a sense of well-being and security. How can this be accomplished?

In our company, we have initiated a personnel planning program that has as its objective the use of normal attrition to level out our employee requirements. We have attrition charts for every location of more than 50 people. Even though Westinghouse's turnover rate is low compared with industry generally, we lose more than 7,000 people a quarter through attrition—that is, from retirements, deaths and resignations, for whatever reason. I receive a report every quarter by business unit on this.

Now, if we plan to modernize a factory that then may require 100 fewer people than it had before, we try to use attrition to accommodate this reduction without any major dislocation of personnel.

This system isn't perfect but it is quite effective. For the last quarter on which we have the report, for example, our losses through attrition came within six people of matching our employee additions, that is new hirees, recalls and the like—a remarkable statistic.

Skillful management can handle the challenge of employment stability in normal times, I believe, if the employment demographics are at all similar to ours. In fact, our company is undergoing major changes right now. It is an unusually active period for plant consolidations, moves, phasing out of old plants and the like. But I believe major corporations are approaching the point where they can voluntarily provide lifelong employment for employees in positions of responsibility. And, in my opinion, achieving employment stability is an obligation of management, not the government.

In addition to the use of attrition techniques, there are some other means of helping to achieve employment stability. Several of our plants now use a cadre of temporary employees—college students, for example, at our Athens, Georgia, plant. This protects the core work force, which might be 80 or 90 percent of the total employment, from layoff in slack times.

It isn't only top management that is concerning itself with

employment security plans. Our plant managers are coming up with different schemes on their own. One manager said to me, "I'll never go through a layoff like I did several years ago." I asked what he was doing about it. Whereupon he explained how his plant sets aside 10 percent of its workload which, in good times, it "offloads" or has done on the outside. The suppliers know that. Then, in bad times, that 10 percent load is brought back into the plant.

If you provide a 10 percent cushion through use of temporary employees and have another 10 percent cushion through use of a work offload system, your plant will have a 20 percent factor to assure employment stability in tough times.

I believe the public should know that management is making these kinds of efforts to provide assured employment to its career people, with the goal of providing lifelong employment for those who want it.

The Japanese have gotten a lot of publicity in recent years about their lifelong employment system. But actually, when you take American pension programs and the like into account, I think we provide more lifelong support for employees than do the Japanese. But we should do more, and I think more is possible.

Quality—A Rallying Point

One thing the Japanese should be thanked for is the renewed emphasis on productivity and quality. American industry, before World War II and for a while thereafter, was the center of quality and led the world in productivity. However, during the '60s and early '70s, American industry's rate of productivity improvement began to slow down, while that of other nations, led by Japan, increased. Of course, a great many of the ideas for productivity improvement and quality control originated in America. But it was the Japanese following the war who took them more seriously and put them into practice wholeheartedly.

American management learned about this the hard way—through head-to-head competition in the world market. Now U.S. industry is making a strong comeback in both productivity and quality.

One thing corporate top management must do, I believe, is

provide the company with a strong rallying point—a common denominator—that cuts across organizational lines. In my company, quality has become that theme. Productivity goes hand-in-hand with quality, of course.

We have taken many of our managers to Japan to see what the competition is doing in terms of quality control and productivity improvement. We took a number of our local union leaders along too. Seeing is believing.

We also established a Productivity and Quality Center with a vice-president at its head to assist the entire company in this area. And we have formed some 2,000 Quality Circles throughout the company to bring our employees into the improvement effort.

A key to productivity achievement, as I see it, is to quantify needs and to set specific improvement goals. If top management does a good strategic planning job, looking perhaps five years ahead, and outlines the financial expectations of the corporation, then you can discover what productivity gains must be made to reach those objectives.

In our case, the necessary corporate productivity gain came out to 6 percent per year. In other words, as we did our strategic planning, we found that it required at least a 6 percent productivity gain each year to get where we expected to be at the end of the five years. That enabled us to set a specific goal. The number didn't just come out of the air.

Some companies set their sights too low and then miss opportunities to achieve higher goals. You have to quantify your needs. There are a lot of ways to do this. One way is to find out how well your competitors are doing. It's surprising how much you can learn about your worldwide competitors in a completely legal and ethical manner. Read their literature, examine their products. Study 10-Ks. It is important to know what you are competing against.

The CEO and the Board of Directors

Knowledge about the competition isn't the only kind of knowledge top management needs, of course. When the winds of change blow, it is essential to have access to a breadth of knowledge about the world outside the corporate realm. This is the role of the chairman as well as the board of directors.

The kind of a board a chief executive wants varies with the individual, I am sure, but I prefer a board that is small enough—12 to 14 people—to make it possible for me to interface directly with each one. This is because I not only meet with them at the regular meetings but I also use them individually as sounding boards for ideas. Seldom does a month go by that I don't pick up the phone and call one or two directors to get their ideas on important matters I have under consideration.

Of course the CEO has to manage the corporation. That's not the board's function. But the board members provide a broad range of knowledge and experience that no one CEO could possibly possess.

We want a blend of backgrounds on the board, top executives of corporations who know the markets and industries we serve. Because we are a transnational corporation, we try to have board members with some knowledge of world affairs. And it is helpful to have several members from academia. They help stimulate original thinking.

I have an obligation to keep the board members as well informed as possible about the activities of the corporation—both good news and bad news. And a close working relationship is desirable. We recently took our board out of town for two days and went over our long-range strategic plans with them. This was mutually advantageous.

At Westinghouse, we have only one in-house director. Some companies have more than that. My reason for limiting the number of in-house directors is that such a person has a very difficult time being truly independent. It would be most unusual for any inside director to oppose a CEO's desired action. I would be most uncomfortable in that position.

Of course it is essential that the top management group knows everything that goes on in the board meetings. So our management committee members sit in on all the board meetings. Some of them also sit in on board committee meetings. And nearly all of the management committee members make presentations to the board from time to time on their parts of the business.

Surprise Insurance and Shock Absorbers

How many times have you heard top executives plead for "no surprises?" Well, I know of only one way to avoid the big surprise and the sudden shock—stay informed. Easier said than done, perhaps. But it's mainly a question of being involved in the decisions that are made when major actions are taken.

I use the term "comfort level" when referring to the degree of knowledge I want about any important activity going on in the company. For example, I spend a lot of time getting an understanding of any proposed acquisition. I want to feel comfortable that I fully understand its implications before I "sign the check," so to speak.

Another way you can put a shock absorber under your desk is to hedge your bets. Don't "bet the farm" on any one proposition, no matter how good it might look on paper. Sometimes things will go awry no matter how well the homework is done. Much depends on the track record of the individual who is proposing a particular project. If his or her record is good, there is a high probability that this recommended project or acquisition also will be good.

Essentially, it's the free flow of information, back and forth, that establishes a high comfort level between the members of management and the CEO. It is my responsibility to get them to want to involve me in their plans. That means we have good two-way communications established.

Consequently, I do not hesitate to talk directly to a division manager, for example, to get information and a better understanding of a particular problem. It is not necessary for me to go through organization channels. Everybody knows this is the way I like to operate. But I don't give orders that way—I do not bypass logical levels of management.

TODAY AND THE FUTURE

There are some people to whom you can delegate a job and think no more about it. There are others with whom you need to stay in touch. Both may be equally capable of getting the job done, but they work differently. You have to understand their differences.

This is particularly important in running a decentralized company such as Westinghouse. When George Westinghouse headed the company he had one basic business to oversee. He had relatively few plants and offices and he undoubtedly made all the major decisions.

The situation today is quite different. As I said, we have 30 separate and largely self-sufficient business units. They are responsible for developing their own business strategies and reaching their own objectives. They exist as free-standing, independent companies to the greatest extent possible.

The chief executive must also be sensitive to the capabilities and limitations of the people on his management team. I consider this extremely important, particularly when delegating control. Obviously, different executives have different gifts, different skills. The CEO shouldn't ask singles hitters to hit home runs, nor should he suggest that the most creative management people spend their time on the day-to-day managing of the business. Some years ago, our company assigned one of its most creative engineers to the post of general manager of a big new plant. He not only failed to manage the plant well, he was lost as a creative force in the company—a terrible waste of talent.

My interest in staying in direct touch with key people in the organization has the additional advantage of helping to prevent such poor executive assignment. The better I know key people personally, the less likely I will be to estimate incorrectly their potential for assignment to greater or different responsibilities.

And, in the final analysis, the CEO can be confident of a corporate structure—comprised of an effective management team—that can handle successfully the predictable and unpredictable changes that face every corporation in both the near and far-reaching future.

George Weissman

George Weissman is chairman of the executive committee of the board of directors of Philip Morris, Inc. During his tenure as chairman and chief executive officer (1978-84) the operating revenues of Philip Morris nearly doubled from their previous level, net earnings grew by 121 percent, to $903.5 million, and dividends increased by 183 percent.

A pioneer in advocating and cultivating corporate social responsibility, Mr. Weissman enlarged his company's 15-year program in support of the arts to include its historic sponsorship of "The Vatican Collections: The Papacy and Art." He also served as general chairman of Summer Jobs '83, a program of the New York City Partnership, Inc., which mobilized the private sector to provide jobs for nearly 20,000 economically disadvantaged young people.

Mr. Weissman is a board member of Gulf & Western Industries, Chemical New York, Corporation and Chemical Bank, Avnet, Inc., and the Business Committee for the Arts. He is a vice-chairman of Lincoln Center and a trustee of the Whitney Museum of American Art. In 1984 Governor Mario Cuomo appointed Mr. Weissman head of a citizens' advisory committee which suggests ways to strengthen the economy of the State of New York.

6
OUTSIDER
POWER

By George Weissman
Chairman of the Executive Committee
of the Board of Directors
Philip Morris, Inc.

These are lessons from a rag-to-riches story—a classic American tale of a corporate immigrant who came to this country and prospered, the story of a small company which fought the giants and won and is working to continue winning.

When *Fortune* published its list of America's 500 leading industrial companies for the year 1983, Philip Morris ranked 35th in sales ($9,465,600,000)* and 15th in net earnings ($903,500,000). Once just an American offshoot of a British tobacconist, we had accomplished a lot in the 29 years since the first *Fortune* 500 lists, on which we ranked 218th in sales ($143,000,000) and 137th in net earnings ($11,400,000). And we had accomplished even more in the 50 years since 1933, when Philip Morris earned less than $500,000.

For us, 1983 was a landmark. After a 50-year struggle, we moved into first place among the six U.S. cigarette companies. We were the second-largest publicly held cigarette producer in the world and also successful makers of two other products providing simple pleasures—beer and soft drinks. Under our

---

* Total revenues amounted to $12,975,900,000, including $3,510,300,000 in excise taxes on our products, which we collected from our customers and remitted to the U.S. and foreign governments. Revenues in 1984 were $13,813,700,000.

direction, Miller Brewing Company had become the second-largest brewer in the United States and the world, and Miller Lite the best-selling reduced-calorie beer; 7UP is the number-one lemon-lime and caffeine-free soft drink in both the United States and the world. Around the world each day 90 million people use a Philip Morris product.

Our success has certainly involved superior products and marketing, along with careful long-range planning. We also drew strength from successful employee relations and a strong sense of corporate responsibility to society. Yet the dominant theme is simpler: we started as outsiders, and from the beginning had to battle harder and differently than the rest.

This pattern has implications not only for our future but also for other industries. There are advantages to being an outsider that a successful company should never forget. A have-not company has to compensate for its size by discerning and seizing opportunity where others fail to, gaining ground through speed and outflanking its competitors rather than engaging in head-on conflict.

Some say we've had more than our share of breaks. After all, our principal products are agriculturally based, and we can usually count on plentiful, high-quality raw materials at reasonable prices. In addition, cigarettes, beer and soft drinks are low-unit-cost, high-turnover items which millions use daily for enjoyment. The market for all three is resistant to economic downturn. Yet in all of our businesses, we have faced some of the fiercest competitors in all of industry. We still do. So in our experiences are lessons that may be applicable to other consumer-goods businesses as well.

CAPITALIZING ON PEDIGREE

Philip Morris is known for expanding its share of market by creating specialized marketing niches for its products. This was true as far back as 1847 when the original Philip Morris opened a tobacco shop on Bond Street, London. The small firm concentrated on a specialized market—the carriage trade—and in 1901 was awarded a royal warrant as tobacconist to the newly crowned King Edward VII, the first British monarch ever to smoke in public.

Meanwhile, cigarettes with the Philip Morris label were being imported into the United States and, later, manufactured here. In 1919 American stockholders took over the U.S. end of the business.

Although the decade of the '20s was a period of tremendous growth for the U.S. cigarette industry, by 1930 only four brands were accounting for 90 percent of the cigarettes sold: Camel, Lucky Strike, Chesterfield and Old Gold. Each was produced by one of the rather clubby companies created when the giant tobacco trust of James B. Duke was dissolved: R. J. Reynolds, American Tobacco, Liggett & Myers and P. Lorillard.* Yet on a small share of the remainder, tiny Philip Morris managed quite nicely. The veteran tobacco men running it, Reuben M. Ellis and Leonard B. McKitterick, continued to follow the original London strategy of creating a product with an individual quality and image that would stake out a particular market niche.

Their method was to flaunt the English pedigree of Philip Morris, endowing their cigarettes with snob appeal through expensive packings (flat boxes covered with brown paper designed to resemble bamboo wood) and pricing them for the luxury market at 30 cents or more for 20 (the leaders sold at 15 cents). To attract the growing number of women smokers, they introduced a new brand with a lipstick-resistant tip in an elegant white package, priced at 20 cents for 20. Its name, first used 40 years earlier by the Bond Street shop, was Marlborough—but with a difference. To save space and because some Americans pronounced the word to rhyme with "rough," the last three letters were dropped.

CALLING ON OPPORTUNITY

The crash of 1929 created new opportunity in the previously small 10-cents-a-pack segment of the market. Philip Morris staked out a position by acquiring the low-

---

*A fifth cigarette company, smaller than any of the Big Four but much larger than Philip Morris, was Brown & Williamson, the U.S. subsidiary of the London-based British-American Tobacco company. The latter had also been part of the tobacco trust.

priced Paul Jones brand. The subsequent growth of Paul Jones gave the company momentum to move into the 15-cent field where 90 percent of cigarettes were being sold.

In January 1933, at virtually the low point of the Great Depression, Philip Morris took on the powerful brands of the Big Four companies by introducing Philip Morris English Blend. Though the new brand's name capitalized on Philip Morris' traditional upper-crust image and offered a richer taste than the other Big Four blends, in price and pack size it competed with them directly. Hence, Ellis and McKitterick had to be especially alert to make a niche for their brand against such overwhelming odds.

Right at the outset they spotted an opportunity. In those pre-vending-machine days, cigarettes were sold mostly in small cigar stores. As the depression wore on, the Big Four companies kept taking actions that reduced dealers' prices and profit margins. By the time Philip Morris English Blend made its debut, the country's 600,000 tobacco dealers were up in arms.

Philip Morris, whose leaders over the years had been at pains to cultivate friendships with dealers, took advantage of this opening by offering the trade its new brand priced to sell at a firm 25 cents a pack, with an extra-generous margin to the dealer built in. With the company about to be reorganized to include Continental Tobacco in what is now known as Philip Morris, Incorporated, several thousand shares of new stock were earmarked for key dealers at a friendly price of $10 per share.

This careful attention to the distribution chain became a hallmark of the new company that was still evident when I joined Philip Morris years later. Alfred E. Lyon, the chairman at the time, said to me, "Anybody can make cigarettes—not as well as we do, but anybody can. But unless they're sold, nothing else happens. Without the distributors and the retailers, we haven't any business here."

To reinforce its distribution efforts, Philip Morris needed a strong advertising campaign and engaged the services of Milton Biow, an advertising man with a record of success in the powerful new medium of radio. In a company storeroom full of obsolete display material, he ran across a 1919 poster showing a bellboy delivering a package of cigarettes on a silver tray. It carried the caption "Call for Philip Morris."

In print, the four words were an innocuous pleasantry, but Biow thought that the right voice could turn them into a memorable radio slogan. Searching for "the best bellboy in New York City," he and Lyon were directed to the Hotel New Yorker and a young man from Brooklyn named John Roventini. Johnny, as he came to be known, was then 23. Though less than four feet tall, he had a dazzling smile, a cheery manner and a voice of extraordinary carrying power. Biow asked him to page the loungers in the hotel lobby with a "call for Philip Morris." After hearing Johnny's delivery, Biow hired him on the spot.

Within days Johnny was sounding off on the first Philip Morris radio program. In public, passing out samples of the new brand, he appeared in the uniform of a bellboy in a swank Edwardian-era London hotel: scarlet coat with brass buttons and pillbox hat with chin strap. His likeness soon appeared on thousands of window and counter displays which tobacco dealers eagerly put up to stimulate sales of their highest-margin popular-priced brand of cigarettes. Through the power of its combined aural and visual personification by Johnny, the new brand achieved almost instant recognition. He was a living trademark, the first ever.

As the country recovered from the depression, the combination of high-quality product, strong product image, aggressive distribution tactics, premium dealer profit margin and memorable advertising enabled Philip Morris to carve out a growing share of the popular-priced market once reserved by the Big Four. By early 1936, three years after its introduction, the sales of Philip Morris English Blend had reached a level of 3.5 billion units a year—still far below the 30 billion-plus of Camel and Lucky Strike but a potential challenge to the 6.5 billion of Old Gold. Company profits had more than quintupled. The stock offered to tobacco dealers at $10 per share was selling at $70.

Though surrounded by Goliaths, the David that was Philip Morris had not only survived but prospered, thanks to attitudes and ways of doing things which continue to form our company style today.

EXPORTING QUALITY

Despite our success, through the '30s the *ranking* of the principal brands remained unchanged, with Philip Morris English Blend well behind the leaders. To assure further growth, Philip Morris had to penetrate new markets. World War II provided that opportunity.

Shipments of cigarettes to the armed forces tended to consist of a single brand. On a given day, an infantry unit or ship's company might have nothing but Camels on hand, and a few days later nothing but Philip Morris. This caused English Blend to be sampled by hundreds of thousands of smokers who otherwise might never have tried it—and its high quality and rich taste paid off. Many soldiers and sailors found that they preferred our product.

In addition, the wartime presence of American troops overseas introduced millions of foreigners to American cigarettes, which came to be regarded as symbols of American prestige and product quality. As the world recovered from war, those countries began to offer possibilities for export sales.

By then, O. Parker McComas had joined the Philip Morris executive ranks, becoming president in 1949. From Bankers Trust, where before the war he had been executive vice-president for Europe, McComas brought a knowledge of finance, which the company's growth was beginning to require, along with broad experience in doing business internationally. He made use of a far-flung network of sales agents, formed in the days of the Bond Street shop, through which Philip Morris had become a familiar name in most parts of the British Empire. Before long, the American Philip Morris became the first serious exporter of American-made cigarettes.

Any of the Big Four companies could have seized the same opportunity. But they were so large that a few hundred million extra cigarettes in export sales meant little to them, while to Philip Morris it meant a great deal.

CRISIS AND COWBOYS

By the early '50s Philip Morris had started to advertise

English Blend on television. We became the original sponsor of "I Love Lucy," probably the greatest long-term success of all TV shows. Sales were surging so strongly that we built additions to both of our cigarette plants, in Richmond and Louisville. At that point, cigarettes became the center of a public controversy.

The crisis was triggered by publication in *The Reader's Digest* of a series of articles alleging a relationship between cigarette smoking and cancer. While the cigarette companies firmly believed that the charges were not scientifically proven, they nevertheless determined to underwrite research on smoking and health, and in 1953, under the leadership of Parker McComas, formed the independent Tobacco Industry Research Committee. Since then, the American tobacco industry has contributed more than $120,000,000 for independent research into the possible effects of cigarette smoking on human health.

Meanwhile, the charges were headline news and jolted millions of smokers into profoundly changing their attitude toward the handful of major brands which had dominated the U.S. cigarette market for so long. This faced tobacco companies with two related marketing problems: how to maintain consumer loyalty to their traditional products and at the same time develop one or more new products—filter-tip—which would attract the smokers seeking an alternative.

As the latter rapidly became an urgent necessity, McComas and Alfred Lyon devised two approaches. One involved merger—a step which would immediately diversify the product line while spreading the expense of creating new products. Soon Philip Morris acquired the American Benson & Hedges, a small cigarette company of English origin with much the same background as Philip Morris (Bond Street shop, carriage-trade products) whose luxury brands offered good possibilities for mass-market exploitation.

One was Parliament, a premium-priced filter cigarette which Philip Morris eventually turned into a high-prestige, popular-priced filter brand through marketing emphasis on its unique recessed filter. The Benson & Hedges name in time became the basis of another major brand. In a sense the merger turned out to be a reverse takeover, for it introduced into the high command of Philip Morris an extraordinarily gifted and dynamic Benson & Hedges executive, Joseph F. Cullman III who subsequently succeeded Lyon and McComas and headed the company for 21 years.

COWBOY COMPETITION

Even before the merger, Philip Morris had a second plan: to revamp an obscure holdover from the '20s, endowing it with a fresh set of psychological associations. The holdover was Marlboro.

The new Marlboro broke completely with its English pedigree. Using the richest blend of tobacco available, we remade it into a full-flavored filter cigarette with a strongly American, masculine image (cork tip; bold red, white and black package). As an additional incentive to get the brand talked about and tried, we introduced the first new cigarette package seen in years, the Flip Top box.

Launched on television with a catchy jingle ("You get a lot to like with a Marlboro—filter, flavor, Flip Top box"), the new brand faced formidable competition. Without the Flip Top box to make a difference, in the early going Marlboro might well have been swamped by L&M, Kent, Viceroy and, above all, Winston, introduced by the industry's largest company, R.J. Reynolds. With features much like Marlboro's, Winston also was promoted with a memorable jingle: "Winston tastes good, like a cigarette should." Backed by greater distribution and marketing muscle than any other brand could muster, Winston soon became the number-one filter cigarette.

Yet, over the long term, Marlboro managed not only to catch up but move into first place. It is still increasing its lead. The most telling factor in this upset has been the gradual evolution of its brand image.

Coupled with the "filter, flavor, Flip Top box" theme, the first advertisements for Marlboro featured a handsome, muscular man, occasionally with a woman. Sometimes he was a lumberjack, sometimes an athlete, sometimes a cowboy, sometimes a sophisticate in white tie and tails. On the back of one hand could be seen a tattoo—an image inspired by a remark attributed to Jack London: "Follow any man with a tattoo and you will find a romantic and adventurous past." It wasn't entirely a coincidence that to some of us in the company these images suggested Philip Morris itself, the outsider who came up the hard way.

Many advertising campaigns keep adding elements in an attempt to widen their appeal. Marlboro did the opposite. In time, the tattoo went. The women went. In response to concern about the influence of cigarette advertising on young people, the athletes went. Eventually the lumberjacks and telephone lineman also disappeared until only the cowboy remained.

Philip Morris had correctly spotted a new cultural trend. Men and women began wearing jeans and boots, shows like "Gunsmoke" and "Bonanza" grew into long-running television hits, John Wayne became the top male movie star—and Marlboro ads began silhouetting a single cowboy against a distant mountain, along with the phrase "Marlboro Country" and, on television, the crashing chords of the theme from *The Magnificent Seven*.

While the advertisements grew simpler, the product grew more complex, with a traditional soft pack variation, a menthol line extension, a 100 mm. length and eventually a Light version. Yet the simplicity and memorability of the advertising has made it possible to sell all of these different Marlboros, the equivalent of several separate major brands, through a single campaign. Most companies strive for economies of scale in manufacturing or distribution. The Marlboro campaign illustrates what they can mean in advertising.

After 30 years of tinkering and simplifying, an introductory campaign for a new brand evolved into a living legend. Marlboro is now the number-one cigarette in the United States, number one internationally and quite possibly the most frequently used branded product in the world.

BEYOND CIGARETTES

Philip Morris made marketing history with Marlboro despite the furor over smoking and health. But the controversy continued. In 1964 came the Surgeon General's Report, in which the federal government formally took a position against smoking. This was followed in 1966 by the requirement that all packages of cigarettes and cigarette advertising carry a warning label, in 1971 by the ban on broadcast advertising and, in recent years, by regulations to limit or ban smoking in public facilities and places of employment.

Concurrently, ever-mounting taxes on cigarettes, an indirect result of this opposition, have raised prices enough to make some Americans give up smoking. The number of new smokers has gone down. Coupled with a flattening of growth in the U.S. smoking population, these trends have led to some pessimistic forecasts about our industry's future, although in 1984, industry volume rose .6 percent.

At Philip Morris we believe the stability, profitability and fundamental simplicity of the cigarette business make it uniquely desirable. Despite the many charges made against cigarettes—charges we question but whose seriousness we fully appreciate—we are extremely confident about the future of our most important product.

First, according to a study by the Wharton School, tobacco supplies or supports some 2 million jobs paying $30 billion in wages and adds over $2 billion annually to the U.S. balance of payments. Second, tobacco is a unique commodity and smoking is a deep-seated anthropological habit that has given satisfaction to a vast number of people for many centuries. The custom dates back nearly 400 years in American history, fully 6,000 years if you heed the evidence of the Mesopotamians.

Over the centuries, smoking has been vilified, taxed and regularly blamed for almost every ailment known to mankind. Yet the people who enjoy smoking have steadily prevailed over those who oppose it, and the industry which serves them has prospered. As long as cigarettes are a legitimate product that is legal to be sold, we will make and sell them.

Philip Morris therefore has utilized cigarette earnings to magnify the returns for our shareholders from that business. Philip Morris' factories, machinery, quality controls and testing laboratories are the newest in the industry and give us the industry's highest levels of productivity. Our competitors are just beginning to catch up.

In addition, we have continued to underwrite new cigarette products which complement the outlook and emerging lifestyles of identifiable groups of smokers, such as independent-minded women (Virginia Slims). Perhaps most notably, we made the large, long-term R & D investment which achieved the breakthrough of technology required to produce a low-tar cigarette with full tobacco flavor (Merit).

We continue to diversify in cigarettes outside the United States. There, where American cigarettes are widely considered to be in a class by themselves, Marlboro is usually our leading brand, but we also market 140 other brands, some of the most successful of which most Americans have never heard of (Lider, Rubios, Peter Jackson, Muratti Ambassadors). Through subsidiaries, affiliates, licensees, direct exports and other arrangements, Philip Morris brands are sold in more than 170 countries and territories. The revenues of our Philip Morris International operating company, today number two among international cigarette companies, keep growing steadily. Philip Morris also exports nearly 40 billion cigarettes annually—more than half the U.S. total—which, according to *Fortune* magazine, makes us the nation's 14th largest exporter.

Yet from time to time Philip Morris has generated earnings even beyond what it takes to meet all needs in cigarettes. In the late '50s, we used them to acquire the first of the paper-making and packaging companies collectively known as Philip Morris Industrial. In 1972 we acquired Mission Viejo Company, designer and builder of large-scale planned communities in California and Colorado.

In between, we acquired a group of companies that made chewing gum, razor blades and shaving cream, products with the same high-turnover, low-unit-cost characteristics as cigarettes and sold in many of the same outlets. They seemed a natural fit with our management interests and abilities. Then, largely because of Marlboro, our cigarette sales grew so rapidly that the new acquisitions were left far behind. Yet each of them took up almost as much management time and energy as cigarettes did. Forced to conclude that the smaller operations simply were not worth our while, we sold them. But when earnings again began to build up, we profited from that lesson and looked for a diversification opportunity large enough to make a significant impact, as well as one likely to benefit from Philip Morris-style management. In 1969 we found and acquired such a property.

MILLER TIME

The Miller Brewing Company was then 115 years old and something of a have-not, ranking eighth in the U.S. beer industry, far behind the leaders, Anheuser-Busch and Schlitz. As with our pricing and promotion of Philip Morris, our entry into the international cigarette market and our introduction of the Flip Top box, we immediately began looking for ways to outflank the giants.

We set ourselves three tasks. One was to prepare Miller to become a significantly larger factor in the beer industry than it had ever been. Higher sales were a must if we were to recoup our purchase price. We began by spending a great deal of money to give Miller state-of-the-art brewing equipment and quality controls, as well as to enlarge and upgrade the sales force and improve communications and service to distributors.

The second task was to change perceptions of Miller's principal product, High Life, as we had successfully changed perceptions of Marlboro. High Life, advertised as "the champagne of bottled beer," was then thought of as the beer of the country-club set—which isn't much of a market for beer. We had to reposition it for the working man, to widen High Life's acceptance among the 20 percent of beer-drinkers who consume 80 percent of the beer. After careful market research we launched the "Miller Time" campaign, identifying High Life with the satisfaction one feels when a good day's work is done, and put millions of dollars behind it.

The third part of our strategy was to develop a product portfolio for Miller, a family of brands for different market niches like the one Philip Morris already possessed in cigarettes. Miller especially needed an attention-getter that would break the pattern of the traditional beer market.

Remembering the shift of consumer cigarette preference to lighter filter cigarettes, we speculated that substantial numbers of beer-drinkers might be interested in a lighter kind of beer. Unlike some past attempts by other brewers, it had to be good-tasting and persuasively presented. The result was Lite Beer from Miller, with a third fewer calories than regular beer but advertised with a strongly positive thrust ("Everything you've always wanted in a beer. And less."). The now-famous television commercials featuring retired athletes told the world that people who enjoy beer like Lite.

Steeped in tradition, the beer industry scorned Miller and predicted that beer-drinkers would scorn Lite. But it turned out that beer-drinkers *had* been waiting for a product like Lite. The timing was right. But, for our competitors this took months to become clear—and while they waited for Lite to fail, we established it as a success.

Today every major brewer markets lower-calorie beer. It is a separate category of beer, the first ever developed in the New World. By the end of 1984, the category included about 20 percent of all beer consumed in the United States—more than half of it Lite Beer from Miller.

When Philip Morris bought Miller for $227 million, it was said we paid too much. When Miller's sales and operating income languished while we prepared for the future, it was said that cigarette people didn't understand beer.

But over the long term, Miller has gone from eighth to second place in its industry, from 4 percent to about 20 percent in share of market, from under $200 million to almost $3 billion in revenues, and from $11.4 million to as much as $227 million in operating income. Though High Life is experiencing some trouble, Lite and High Life rank second and third among all U.S. beer brands, and our two newest brands, Meister Brau and Milwaukee's Best, are penetrating the market. Strategy and tactics that worked in cigarettes showed they could work elsewhere as well.

SEVEN-UPMANSHIP

Just as the earnings generated by our tobacco operations made possible the acquisition and renewal of Miller, their continuation made possible the acquisition, in 1978, of the Seven-Up Company of St. Louis, Missouri.

Seven-Up presented similar challenges. In the soft-drink industry, it, too, was something of a have-not, an outsider far behind Coca-Cola and Pepsico, the leaders. It was essentially a single-product company (lemon-lime soda) at a time when consumer preference was trending toward variety and choice in soft drinks. And, with colas accounting for roughly 60 percent of the soft-drink market, that single product was out of the industry mainstream.

As with Miller, our first task was to lay the groundwork for Seven-Up to become significantly larger. The reason was the same: to make possible a recouping of our investment, which this time amounted to some $500 million.

Several of the executives who had been instrumental in the success of Miller moved on to Seven-Up. There, as at Miller, they began to enlarge and upgrade the company's plant and equipment, quality controls, sales force, communications and service. Their next task was to increase the sales base through stepped-up advertising, expanded marketing overseas and, above all, strong promotional emphasis on Diet 7UP, an exceptionally good-tasting product which could ride the trend of a growing national concern for physical fitness and weight control.

With these preliminaries out of the way, attention shifted to longer-term questions: how to gain a greater share of the soft-drink market, and whether an opportunity existed for a new-product success on the order of Lite Beer from Miller.

To both questions we came up with a single answer—no caffeine. 7UP contained none and never had, while caffeine was uniformly present in colas. With this product difference as a lever, we hoped to chip off for 7UP a portion of the colas' massive market share. We followed through with a direct challenge to colas, LIKE, the first cola ever to be caffeine-free. Some of the other companies reacted angrily, displaying the same attitude toward playing up no caffeine that the brewers had displayed toward reducing calories in beer. (The media dubbed the advertising battles we provoked the "Cola Wars.") But this time our competitors also took the precaution of countering with their own caffeine-free colas.

Our timing was good. Consumers were ready for a "no caffeine" emphasis, and 7UP sales responded well. Its international sales keep growing. But LIKE was not permitted the same head start over the competition that Lite got. Meanwhile we persist. We are in soft drinks as we are in cigarettes—for the long term.

AN OPEN-DOOR CULTURE

In 1983, when Philip Morris, with a 34.4 percent U.S. market share, moved into first place among the six domestic cigarette companies, it was an exciting moment. As recently as 1960 we had been the smallest of the six, with a combined market share for all our brands of less than 10 percent. Our satisfaction was all the sweeter from knowing that at various times during our run for the roses we had been outclassed in assets, earning power, breadth of distribution and advertising weight.

We think we keep succeeding primarily because we resist complacency, maintaining the "David vs. Goliath" outlook and have-not motivation that helped us succeed in the first place.

A second factor has been our exceptional depth and continuity of management. Philip Morris rarely needs to go outside the company to fill a top position. When our present team of senior executives—chairman, vice-chairman and president—took over in July 1984, they brought to their posts combined experience at Philip Morris of more than 100 years.

Two further factors have contributed—a successful corporate culture and a strong sense of corporate responsibility.

Others frequently comment on our distinctive corporate esprit—a mixture of pride, competitiveness and considerate team play. In part it has arisen because, as outsiders, we have made a point of going outside the standard hiring pool to improve our chances of finding and recruiting superior people at lower levels. Long before legal or social pressures to do so, Philip Morris began hiring women and members of minority groups to fill positions which traditionally had been closed to them. Our search has been not only for trained specialists in the various disciplines of business but also for able and energetic entrepreneurs willing to make themselves specialists in Philip Morris—the kind of men and women who allow us to promote consistently from within.

The quality of our managers can be judged not only by our sales and earnings but by our innovations: the Flip Top box, the recessed filter, 100 mm. cigarettes at popular prices, the first single-digit low-tar cigarette with decent flavor (Merit), the first slim cigarette (Virginia Slims), the first successful lower-calorie beer (Lite), the first beer advertising on the theme of reward-for-work (Miller Time), the first soft-drink advertising on the theme of no-caffeine (7UP), the first U.S. cigarette to become the world's best-seller (Marlboro).

In making decisions, Philip Morris has never followed the hierarchical command structure found so often in large corporations. Our approach is essentially collegial, stemming from the years when the company could house its entire management on one floor of a Manhattan office building and the atmosphere was that of a small business.

In the different circumstances of today, we still encourage our managers to look on each other as colleagues and fellow entrepreneurs. We try to encourage by example. Our top managers still visit the trade, attend marketing conventions and make retail calls. We walk through our factories and sit in on advertising and marketing meetings. Individual offices are small and unintimidating. Doors are mostly kept open. There is heavy stress on keeping employees informed and involved in our moves. Ideas are solicited and evaluated in terms of what they are, rather than where they come from—and, whenever possible, tried. If people of ability and spirit, at whatever level, are not encouraged to speak up and given all the responsibility they can handle, there's no point in hiring them.

RESPONSIBILITY TO SOCIETY

In classical economic theory, the responsibilities of a company operating under the capitalistic system are to produce goods or services, provide jobs, pay taxes and generate earnings for shareholders. At Philip Morris, we have been conscientious about that. But we also are sensitive to the needs of society and the obligation of a strong company like ours to make positive contributions to society's well-being. Since the claims of society and those of shareholders can seem to conflict, serving the interests of both has always been one of our most demanding challenges, as it is for most large and visible companies.

Philip Morris defined its long-standing approach to this

issue a number of years ago when we wrote in our annual report: "We expect our business activities to make social sense and our social activities to make business sense." It pleases us that this thought was subsequently adopted almost word for word by The Business Roundtable as a recommendation for all companies.

That policy has shaped the way we updated and enlarged our facilities. By the late '60s our cigarette factory in Richmond was becoming obsolete. We had to decide whether to build the new plant and research center we needed within the city limits or move where the land would be cheaper, taxes would be less, and shipments and deliveries wouldn't have to contend with the delays of urban street traffic.

Our decision was to stay. While we were at it, we set out to erect buildings of architectural distinction. Our Richmond Manufacturing Center, designed by Gordon Bunshaft, has been called the most beautiful factory in America. People enjoy working there and Richmond takes great pride in it.

We made the same kind of decision in the late '70s when Philip Morris was starting to burst out of its headquarters offices in New York City. At a time when many other companies were hitting the road to the suburbs, we acquired a parcel of land across the street from Grand Central Terminal and erected our own building, designed by Ulrich Franzen. To bring a unique amenity to one of the world's busiest street locations, we provided rent-free space on the ground floor for a branch of the Whitney Museum of American Art. It is often described as one of the most successful spaces of its kind in the city.

Why did we expand within Richmond and New York, and at our cigarette plant in Louisville, at the main Miller brewery in Milwaukee and at Seven-Up headquarters? First, Philip Morris had grown and prospered in those cities. We felt an obligation to them. Second, in each we had thousands of resident employees and many more thousands of loyal customers committed to using the products of a local enterprise. For Philip Morris to abandon those people would be turning our backs on our strongest supporters. Third, the United States depends on cities and city life for much of its variety and vitality. Yet most U.S. cities, including the ones important to Philip Morris, were experiencing declines in population and economic strength. We believed that for a strong and successful company like ours to add to their decline would be morally wrong and in the long run bad for both the country and our company, while staying to build or rebuild would be the reverse.

This policy is an example of business activities that make social sense. And in selecting locations for the *new* plants we needed, we were guided by such purely economic considerations as land costs, availability of labor, prospective taxes and proximity to raw materials and markets, which is why Philip Morris' newest cigarette factory is in tobacco country near Charlotte, North Carolina, and our new breweries are in such communities as Fulton, New York, Albany, Georgia and Irwindale, California.

A second example of social activities that make business sense is Philip Morris' pace-setting corporate support of the arts. Over the last 20 years, frequently in partnership with the National Endowment for the Arts, the company has underwritten more than 100 important art exhibitions in the United States and nearly as many abroad. The most celebrated is one of the most recent—237 works of art from the Vatican Collections, which early in 1984 completed a year-long tour to the leading museums of New York, Chicago and San Francisco.

This sponsorship makes possible exhibitions which could not have been mounted without it and has returned a twofold benefit to society. Millions of Americans have been enriched through seeing great works of art with their own eyes. Meanwhile, in an era of sharply rising costs, many of our leading museums of art have received much-needed assistance through the revenues which important exhibitions generate. We're proud that the chairman of the board of the Metropolitan Museum of Art could recently tell the *New York Times*: "This is the first year in a while that we have not run at a deficit, and that is because of the Vatican show."

As with the social sense, the business sense in art sponsorship means a lot to us. One perquisite of sponsoring an exhibition is the right to a private preview of one's own. We use such occasions to entertain people who are important to Philip Morris—members of the financial community, customers and suppliers, public officials and other dignitaries, and the business and trade press. We also try to sponsor exhibitions that will travel to one or more of the cities and towns where we have plants or offices, in which case we arrange special previews for Philip Morris employees.

Yet the most important business benefits we receive are intangible and cumulative. As a company of managers and marketers, we find that our corporate interest in art stimulates us to look in new and even daring ways at our creative efforts—packaging, promotion and advertising—all critical to our success. It affects our attitudes and alertness toward the world in general as well, enhancing Philip Morris' ability to communicate daily with vast numbers of people in an era of increasingly sophisticated and complex visual language.

Finally, for a company to sponsor great art is to associate itself with quality on the grand scale. That Philip Morris, maker of commonplace products like cigarettes and beer, also cares about the beautiful and noble achievements of civilization, highlights something about our company that is uniquely positive. In addition to making employees and shareholders proud, it demonstrates a commitment to society's highest values which I believe a public often suspicious of business respects and may even admire.

A third area where our business and social activities came together is that of social welfare. Like many other companies, Philip Morris supports good causes generously and with enthusiasm, and strongly encourages our employees to contribute volunteer time.

Some of our people also work closely on behalf of the company with black and Hispanic organizations—partly because our principal installations are in large cities and partly because cigarettes, beer and soft drinks, though enjoyed by consumers of all kinds, are pleasures that poor people can afford, and members of minorities are users of our products in greater proportions than their representation in the population.

Such common interests with minority communities long ago led Philip Morris to become a significant depositor in banks owned by minorities and women. We have a program to guide and assist minority firms seeking to become Philip Morris suppliers. We contribute financially to many minority-based organizations, with special emphasis on those concerned with education and job training.

Long term, these activities are good for society. They also help the sale of our products. I will add that Philip Morris is particularly proud of them. We are happy indeed to be among the haves. We fought hard to become one. But we know what it can mean to be a have-not.

THE LONG TERM FROM NOW

When people ask me about the future of Philip Morris, I cite the following statistics:

At the end of 1984, Philip Morris controlled only 35.3 percent of the U.S. cigarette market and 6.4 percent of the international market. We controlled only 20.2 percent of the U.S. beer market and 6.2 percent of the U.S. and Canadian soft-drink market. Though Philip Morris has come a long way, there is plenty of opportunity for us to go a lot farther. It seems reasonable to expect that our increasing strength will lead to still further increases in market share.

I said at the beginning that this was a rags-to-riches story. If Ernest Hemingway hadn't already used the title for one of his novels, I might have called it *To Have and Have Not*.

Instead, let me suggest a moral borrowed from Irving Berlin, who, like Philip Morris, arrived as an immigrant and went on to success in the mass market. Berlin said: "The toughest thing about success is that you've got to keep on being a success. Talent is only a starting point. In this business you've got to keep on working that talent."

It's the same in our business—and that's what Philip Morris intends to keep on doing.

William G. McGowan

William G. McGowan is chairman and chief executive officer of MCI Communications Corporation, a full-service telecommunications company with 1984 sales of almost $2 billion.

Mr. McGowan founded MCI in 1968 with three employees. The company now employs more than 10,000 people and provides a full range of worldwide voice, data and message delivery and personal communications services to more than 2 million customers.

Recognized by *Time* magazine in its 1984 "Man of the Year" issue as one of seven "pioneers in the best American tradition: inventive, bold, resolute, eager to overcome the challenges that face them," Mr. McGowan was also cited in early 1985 by *Business Week* among its "Business Week 50" of corporate leaders and innovators. He also received an Award of Merit for Distinguished Entrepreneurial Leadership in American Business in 1985 from the Wharton School of the University of Pennsylvania.

Prior to founding MCI, Mr. McGowan was a management and financial consultant, concentrating in high-technology industries.

Mr. McGowan holds an M.B.A. degree from the Harvard Graduate School of Business, where he was a Baker Scholar for academic excellence. He received a B.S. degree from King's College in his native Wilkes Barre, Pennsylvania. Mr. McGowan also is a member of the board of governors of the National Association of Security Dealers (NASD).

MCI's stock (symbol: MCIC) is traded over the counter, and

for the past four years has been the most actively traded issue on the NASDAQ national market system.

7
INFORMATION AGE TECHNOLOGY—
THE COMPETITIVE ADVANTAGE

By William G. McGowan
Chairman
MCI Communications Corporation

I'm glad to have this opportunity to sit back and take the long view toward management in the 1990s. And as I look out over the business landscape, whether it's around me at the growing telecommunications industry or at other industries and their markets, I see common patterns of change. These changes are so sweeping that, not surprisingly, many business observers are speaking in terms of a new age—the information age.

We are all participants in this new rapidly changing era, which is being brought about by the emergence of new computer, telecommunications and information technologies.

These new technologies are creating vast new opportunities and new markets in industry after industry—manufacturing, wholesaling, retailing, finance, insurance and a host of new service suppliers.

The information technologies are changing the structure of markets themselves, and altering the life cycles of products in those markets. They're reordering production and distribution patterns. And they're causing major changes in the structure of our organizations and in the way people work.

As I see it, preparing for the information age, and staying competitive in it, is the single most significant management challenge of our time. Companies and individuals who position themselves to take full advantage of the information technologies will gain the competitive edge. Those who do not risk being left behind.

A LOOK AT THE TELECOMMUNICATIONS INDUSTRY: OPPORTUNITIES ABOUND

In 1968, when MCI was founded, the telecommunications environment in this country was a lot simpler than it is today.

Basically, there were the three industries that made up the system known as the phone company: the local exchanges, the phone equipment industry, and the interexchange long distance industry. There were also telex and cable systems, but the vast majority of traffic was voice traffic, carried by phone lines.

Today, we have competition in both equipment manufacture and long distance communication. The communications infrastructure has expanded its capacity dramatically, incorporating digital microwave, satellite and optical fiber technologies capable of handling not only voice but also huge quantities of image, text, data and video transmission. Customers now have a dazzling array of products and services to choose from, including new generation PBX's that will transmit both data and voice throughout an organization, electronic mail services that carry messages from person to person and computer to computer across the globe, cellular radio systems, audio and video teleconferencing, and much, much more.

Certainly, MCI is changing. No longer just a domestic long distance company, we now offer a full range of communications services in the forms of programmable private line networks, MCI Mail and worldwide message delivery service, international voice and data communication, local communications systems, and packet switching networks.

Through a combination of technology and competition, we've entered a new era in telecommunications, with such amazing statistics as a 9 percent compounded annual growth in domestic voice, a 15 percent compounded annual growth in international voice, and a data communications market expected to grow somewhere between 20 and 50 percent a year for the rest of this decade.

TELECOMMUNICATIONS PLUS: THE LINKUP WITH COMPUTERS AND DATA SERVICES

Paralleling the development in telecommunications has been an awesome progression in computers. They're becoming less and less expensive and more and more powerful all the time. The first commercial computer, ENIAC, was the size of a room. ENIAC operated with 18,000 constantly overheating vacuum tubes, and cost over $3 million to build. A machine of comparable capacity today would be the size of a typewriter and cost under $300. Put another way, if the automobile industry had progressed as much, a Rolls Royce would cost $2.50 and get a million miles to the gallon.

The data services industry has also been expanding. At the end of 1984 there were an estimated 2,400 publicly available data bases in existence. That number is expected to increase more than 40-fold by the end of 1987. An anticipated 8 million homes will be linked into computerized information systems by 1990. A decade ago, just about the only information available electronically to aid decision making was generated by a company's internal data processing department.

And now an even greater change is occurring. The lines separating the telecommunications, computer and data services industries are starting to blur. Already, the technology exists to allow information to be collected, processed and stored virtually anywhere in the world, and then be sent immediately virtually anywhere else for retrieval or further processing.

This increasing capability is the driving force behind the new information age. The technology is here. The communications infrastructure is rapidly falling into place (MCI is currently investing approximately $1 billion a year in its telecommunications network.) A vast quantity of information can be available where we want it, when we want it, and how we want it. All that remains is for managers to understand the transformation that's taking place, and position their companies to take advantage of it.

And that's beginning to happen as well.

DOING BUSINESS IN THE ELECTRONIC MARKETPLACE

Among the most profound business changes that I see occurring now and in the decade to come is a dramatic repositioning of companies in the marketplace. Innovative companies are using the competitive edge that the information technologies provide to create new lines of business, enter new markets, expand their access to existing markets and create new value-added services that increase customer loyalty. They are doing all this in a marketplace that is itself changing because of the technologies that are being introduced. Some examples follow.

Rapid entry into new markets and new lines of business. A few years ago, Citicorp was a large bank. Now it's an international financial services system. Merrill Lynch was a brokerage firm. Now it's also providing banking services and much more. American Express provided cash and credit for travelers. Now it's merchandising everything from tulip bulbs to long distance services. Sears was a retailer. Now it's also in the real estate and financial brokerage businesses, and it's moving into banking and expanding its credit card services. As former Citibank Chairman Walter Wriston says, "Information about money has become almost as important as money itself."

Management's concentration on information has made possible the rapid moves by these companies into new areas of business. In each of these companies, I suspect that at least one highly placed executive will confide that he or she really is in the "information" business. Money, stock, services and products are only the secondary means by which the real profits are made. Information is the competitive advantage.

Use of technology to expand market share. American Hospital Supply is one of a number of companies that are providing their customers on-site order entry systems to alter their distribution patterns and at the same time expand market share. AHS installed a terminal in each of its large customers' hospitals, eliminating the need to have salespeople call on each hospital, collect an order and enter it into the company's data base. With a terminal, the hospital could enter its own order directly, saving the hospital time, and AHS money.

But AHS didn't stop there. They said to the hospitals, "In addition to entering your orders for materials directly into our data base, why don't you also maintain your in-house inventory free of charge on our computer?"

Now that service didn't cost AHS much at all, but it built a lot of goodwill—and helped AHS better predict demand.

Next AHS added another feature. They said to the hospitals, "Why don't you enter all of your orders on our computer. If we can't supply what you want, we'll pass the order on directly to other suppliers."

That strategy has helped AHS build its market share. On the surface, the AHS system might simply seem to be a remote order entry network. But to the executives of AHS, it's a strong, competitive, profit-making tool.

Expansion and shifting of product lines. Other companies are introducing flexible manufacturing systems to improve the efficiency of other manufacturing operations, or to diversify production. General Motors' Saginaw steering gear plant now makes 5,000 separate products, creating them on demand without the need for extensive retooling and John Deere's new flexible manufacturing system at its Waterloo Tractor Works allows parts to be computer designed and computer manufactured on demand.

On Deere's factory floor, machining and assembly are guided by a host computer that gives orders to 10 minicomputers. Foremen monitor progress on 130 terminals tied to the minicomputers.

Shortening of product life cycles. The ability to shift production rapidly is likely to become even more important as we move further into the information age. Product life cycles are becoming much shorter. The IBM personal computer, for example, was developed in less than a year, and we have already seen the introduction of such further refinements as the PC XT and the PC AT. The video-game market developed and matured and declined in about three years.

New products are estimated to provide one third of businesses' profits in the 80s, as compared to about one-fifth in the '70s. In this kind of environment, businesses must maintain close contact with their customers and play close attention to changes in customer demand. This process, too, is aided significantly by the information technologies.

Monitoring of sales and inventory to provide marketing advantage. One way that innovative firms are taking the pulse of the market is through the introduction of point-of-sale systems. B. Dalton Booksellers, for example, tracks sales in its stores by computer not only to provide ongoing inventory control but to predict the kinds of titles that will sell well in each outlet.

Tandy Corporation has a small computer in each of its 8,000 stores, linked by telecommunications to its headquarters in Texas. Top management knows on a daily basis how each store, each product and each merchandising strategy is doing.

Store managers and senior managers in these companies have a direct line to the marketplace. Their use of the information technologies is giving them "early warning" of any shifts in customer buying patterns, an instant reading on the success of an ad campaign and a strong competitive advantage.

Entering the electronic marketplace. How does a firm go about moving into the electronic marketplace? The answer will be different in each industry, of course, but I can give you an MCI example.

In February 1983, we decided to investigate using the information technologies to enter a new market. We pulled together a small group of people who had demonstrated a creative and entrepreneurial style at other companies and said to them: "You create your own organization and develop a new business. Develop it with our money, with our blessing, and with our review."

Nine months later, helped by existing MCI operations and support from outside talents, ranging from Hewlett Packard, Digital Equipment, Bolt, Beranek and Newman, Racal Telesystems and American Management Systems, MCI introduced a new business on schedule and on budget.

The budget was $40 million. The service was MCI Mail.

MCI Mail is the electronic equivalent of the postal service. Messages can be sent computer to computer instantly, and are stored upon arrival in an "electronic in-box." Or MCI will store customers' letterheads, signatures and mailing lists, and deliver paper copies within four hours to addressees who don't have a computer.

MCI Mail incorporates a number of special features. Subscribers can call up the latest stock quotations using the Dow Jones News/Retrieval service. And they can add additional custom features as well. The MCI Mail system we use internally, for example, incorporates an "electronic newsflash" feature. Key news items our staff should be aware of are summarized each day and disseminated electronically throughout the organization.

By applying the information technologies—computers, telecommunications and information—MCI has entered a new market. And we're finding that the service we've developed is an increasingly essential tool in our company's internal communications as well.

WITHIN THE ORGANIZATION— EFFECTS ON JOBS AND PEOPLE

Important as changes in production and distribution patterns and marketing and sales strategies may be, I think that the information age is bringing about an even more profound set of changes—a massive restructuring of the kinds of jobs people do and the way people do them. Use of the information technologies is not only increasing the speed and cost efficiency of communication, but, more important, is changing the way information flows within the organization. That can translate into an enormous opportunity to simplify management structure and improve management's ability to make informed, rational decisions. Managed properly, information technologies can yield dramatic improvements in operating efficiency, worker productivity and the quality of decision making—with a visible impact on the bottom line.

Increases in the speed and cost efficiency of communication. Once an organization is linked up electronically, data can be captured, stored and processed anywhere in the organization, and the resulting information can be communicated anywhere—or everywhere—else. At MCI, for example, we've created a nationwide electronic network that is dramatically increasing our capability to sell to and service our customers. We have close to 5,000 terminals on the network, all over the country, linked by telecommunications lines to data processing centers that are interconnected and strategically placed around the country.

The system helps us in a number of ways. First, it allows us to target who it is we want to reach and then contact them. Our telemarketers don't have to search for phone numbers—the numbers are dialed automatically, from a computer-selected list of likely prospects.

The system also enables sales and order entry staff around the country to process new customers directly into our on-line customer data base. Processing a new customer account used to take days. Now the transaction takes less than four seconds.

If customers have a question or a problem, our customer service representatives can access the customer's file instantly, using either the customer's name or phone number.

We even have an on-line system to manage the network itself. Through our centrally located network management system we know exactly what's taking place on every part of our communications network every second of the day. We know how many transactions are taking place during any given period of time in any city, in any office, and on any terminal. We know how long it should take and does take to process any given transaction. And we can break the time down into the number of seconds or fractions of a second at the sending terminal, on the telecommunications network and in the central processor.

Information technology also provides an efficient and low cost way to store and retrieve information. At MCI we're finding that our electronic files are far less cumbersome than file cabinets, and a file in Washington can, for example, be accessed by an employee in San Francisco.

The cost savings that can be derived from sending messages electronically are considerable. Most companies in the United States today pay an average of over $15 per year for each square foot of office space. We pay to air condition the file cabinets in the summer and heat them in the winter. That's billions of tons of paper being heated and air conditioned, not to mention copied and distributed and mailed and opened and redistributed. We haven't completely eliminated filing cabinets at MCI. But we have cut down on both paper flow and paper storage.

We're also finding that electronic messaging is helping our managers improve their efficiency. For one thing, it's helping to eliminate "telephone tag"—that endless cycle of calling back and forth that takes up so much of busy people's time. For another, particularly in our international division, it's cutting down significantly on the amount of time it takes to communicate. We used to have to allow a week or more to get a letter delivered overseas. Now it's overnight, guaranteed.

Cutting down on management layers. When a company is linked up, data can be entered anywhere in the organization as events occur—as orders are taken, sales are made, monies are disbursed. The data can then be processed any number of ways, and managers can call up the resulting information simply by pressing a key. This means that there is much less need for layers of middle managers in the organization to aggregate and massage that information and pass it along the chain of command.

There are enormous numbers of district managers and group heads in many corporations whose major function is to collect and exchange messages and coordinate the work of other message collectors and message exchangers. Perhaps the greatest gain in efficiency that the introduction of information technologies can bring is the elimination of these excess layers of management in the organization.

There's likely to be a gain in the accuracy of information as well. Managers with "turf" to protect tend to try and present information in its most flattering light. As information gets passed up through the chain of command a certain amount of distortion takes place. I am convinced that the more layers of management you introduce, the less chance you have of anyone—least of all the CEO—really knowing what's going on.

Of course in any organization there's a natural tendency toward empire building that tends to cause the layers of management and staff to proliferate. But at MCI we're working hard to cut down on that. We're constantly working to push decision-making responsibility *down* in the hierarchy and *out* into the field. We're flattening the management pyramid.

That's why MCI Telecommunications decentralized into a divisional structure. MCI Telecommunications now consists of seven regional companies, whose territories coincide with those of the seven Bell regional holding companies. This decentralization is one of the single most far-reaching reorganizations that any company the size of MCI has ever gone through. We are doing it because we believe it is critically important to maintain the organization's flexible, close-to-the-customer decision-making approach.

We're also flattening the management pyramid by allowing numerous "skips" into our corporate hierarchy. At MCI the executive classifications of president, executive vice-president, senior vice-president, director, senior manager and manager all exist, but often a director will report directly to a senior vice-president, a manager will report to a vice-president, or a director will report to a division president.

Looking at the organization chart, it might seem that MCI needs to fill some key staff positions. But in fact, it's our way of getting work done efficiently, without introducing unnecessary layers of management. We believe that the fewer levels of management we have, and the more direct our lines of communication are throughout the organization, the more productive we are.

Improvements in decision making. Information can be a blessing or a curse. Without it, a manager is just guessing blind. But there can also be so much of it that the sheer amount of data, the sheer numbers of choices, paralyzes decision making. Given the vast increases in the amount of information available to managers, I'm sure we'll see some cases of "management information overload" in the next few years.

But we'll also see the development of powerful new aids to decision making. Already managers in innovative companies are using decision support systems not only to call up their latest sales results but also to analyze these results for trends. They're modeling the effects of various alternative responses, and searching into one of a number of data bases for research into demographics, customer buying habits or the state of the economy in the region in question.

In the future we can anticipate an even wider use of decision support software to check different spending levels for promotional activity against anticipated sales or prices. Companies will maintain historical data of their own and competing firms' activities as a basis for such projections.

The combination of these kinds of decision support capabilities with the ability almost instantaneously to process and transmit data is allowing decision making to take place more quickly and more precisely than ever before. And as more and more firms develop the capability to reposition themselves quickly, information-age decision making is becoming a competitive necessity.

LOOKING AHEAD: MANAGING FOR THE 1990s

Clearly, all these changes are going to have a major impact on the way companies do business in the years ahead. I think that the successful companies will continue to succeed because their managers understand the importance of the new technologies and position their companies to take advantage of them. And as a result, I think successful companies—and I trust MCI will be one of them—will share some common characteristics.

The successful companies will be lean, mean and linked up. They will use the information technologies not just in the accounting department and the secretarial pool but throughout the organization—including the executive suite. They will seek out ways to simplify the flow of information within the organization, and cut out excess management layers.

They will be agile and flexible. They will aggressively seek out new opportunities, and be willing to innovate, and change.

They will give the customers what they want. They will pay attention to changing customer buying patterns and will supply what their customers want to buy. Markets are becoming increasingly demand driven. More and more, customers are choosing what they want to buy, rather than simply buying what companies are selling. Companies that wish to succeed in the electronic marketplace must be prepared to respond to customers' needs with new products and custom services—or watch their competitors do so.

MEETING THE CHALLENGE

So how do managers prepare to meet the challenge? I think the first step is to meet the challenge of the technology itself. Infusing an organization with the information technologies is not easy. Resistances must be overcome.

The first line of resistance is a reluctance to view information technologies as a competitive tool rather than an administrative cost. Accounting departments like to see a neat justification for an expenditure in terms of person-hours of time saved or materials not purchased. But the real value of the information technologies is strategic, not administrative. They should be expensed, I think, as part of the direct cost of doing business.

The second line of resistance is people's reluctance to use the new technologies. Some people may fear that a machine could replace them. Others, and there are a good number of these in the executive suite, are simply not comfortable with computers and electronic communication devices. This reluctance can and should be overcome through education and training.

The third line of resistance is an unwillingness to innovate—and keep on innovating. Once a system is in use, people tend to see it as cast in stone. But the companies that gain the advantage are those that are willing to look for new ways to use information systems once they're in place.

It all boils down to developing a willingness to change. The information age is new ground, still very much unexplored. The old maps aren't going to help us, and the old ways of doing things are going to have to be revised. It's a time of great opportunity, but only for those who dare to try.

Even in today's "high-tech" world of rapid change, history repeats itself. Success in the future will depend, just as it always has, on the leadership of CEOs and their key executives, and their willingness to capitalize on the tools available to attain the competitive edge.

T. Mitchell Ford

T. Mitchell Ford, chairman and chief executive officer, Emhart Corporation, has presided over the emergence of this one-time domestic company into a multinational enterprise with nearly $2 billion in revenues ('84), doing business in more than 130 countries annually, via manufacturing operations in the United States and 29 countries abroad.

From an early start as a country lawyer (Lakeville, Connecticut) with a brief legal stint at the CIA, Ford quickly moved up the corporate ranks, despite, he confesses, no M.B.A. degree or financial or accounting credentials.

As a liberal arts undergraduate with a major in sociology, Mr. Ford has been sensitive to the difficulties of communications between people and the impact on corporate credibility, a fragile value and a profound concern to any CEO.

Mr. Ford is a graduate of Hotchkiss, Harvard and Yale Law.

8
CREDIBILITY AND COMMUNICATIONS— CATALYSTS TO EFFECTIVE MANAGEMENT

By T. Mitchell Ford
Chairman and Chief Executive Officer
Emhart Corporation

In corporate reality, the bottom line is credibility!

It's what sustains you when earnings go sour. It's what brings things into proper perspective when times are good. It is the psychological value that shapes the corporate culture, creates the unity every chief executive strives to achieve. It calms and quiets the shareholders, generates support among the financial community, gives the board pride in its membership, builds loyalty among customers, attracts the new, fresh talent every company needs. In short, it is the sine qua non of successful, productive leadership of any company.

I know because in my 14 years as chief executive I have experienced the rewards and the disappointments that this generally elusive, always fragile virtue contributes.

I have also learned, occasionally the hard way, that the key to achieving credibility is understanding how opinions are formed, why facts are not *the* primary determinant. I've learned instead that it is the perception of these facts that creates the support, or the opposition—the credibility or the skepticism about a company, both as it's viewed from outside the corporate walls and from within.

EMHART FROM THE OUTSIDE

At Emhart, our mission is "to earn consistently superior financial returns through the pursuit of a leadership position in the company's businesses." In the long run, we further state our objective to create "value" for the company's shareholders.

These are fine goals. But they take on shape and substance only when—and if—the shareholders and the financial community see and evaluate our record in this context. How they assess the added value we build may differ markedly from our own assessment and, indeed, may differ from the facts. As chief executives, we have to be sensitive to this imbalance and address it. If the public believes its perceptions to be factual, these perceptions have, indeed, become the facts.

Agonizing hand wringing over the ignorance of shareholders or of the financial community is no substitute for taking some perhaps unaccustomed initiative to create credibility when it's lacking.

This leads chief executives into some uncomfortable areas. It may mean speaking and writing more plainly, without the literary escape clauses the lawyers instinctively build into any document. It may mean publicizing bad news as promptly as your staff trumpets the good news. (This certainly goes against the grain. Almost all of us involuntarily withdraw from the unpleasant. It's a natural, human tendency.) It may mean taking the initiative to report or explain some action or policy before being asked to do so. But, as many have learned, a nickel's worth of spunk and candor is worth a million dollars' worth of self-serving corporate advertising in terms of creating credibility.

Each of us, no doubt, can recall many occasions when some outsiders have had a misinformed or distorted view of corporate activities. In our own case, we have had some very tangible evidence of the impact of our own lapses in credibility.

Some years ago we were concerned that our stock price seemed to ignore our performance. There was, we felt, no rational reason for this, even acknowledging that we are fundamentally a conservative, low-visibility company and that our stock is certainly not one the market follows with any animated priority.

Then we factored in some unusual developments—the "surprises" Wall Street abhors. It seemed that over the period in question, we had created a surprise or two a year. Once it was the sudden announcement of a multi-million-dollar write-off caused by a major technological problem we'd not anticipated nor reported. On another occasion, we aborted a much-publicized merger at the eleventh hour—without adequate explanation. Once we ourselves were surprised by a $26 million foreign currency transaction. Then two of our top executives resigned, again without clear-cut explanation on our part, although the reasons were normal and reflected no internal schisms. Finally, just to show we were as bad at handling good news as bad, we produced a fourth quarter one year that was substantially better than had generally been anticipated, or that we had signaled. We had not prepared Wall Street for the good news, which is as important as alerting them to the bad.

Mind you, during this two-and-a-half-year period, we had very good results—record years, in fact.

But it was clear to me that there was a correlation between our soft image on the Street and the fact that we had committed the unpardonable sin; we had become unpredictable and so turned off our friends. Not only had we embarrassed our supporters by these sudden, unexplained surprises but we had also neglected to explain in a timely and reasonable manner why they had occurred.

It is only fair to point out that in a couple of the instances cited we were prevented from commenting for legitimate legal and personal reasons. There will, of course, always be times when the theoretical course of action just isn't feasible. So you have to hunker down and ride it out.

But that does not gainsay the critical importance of fighting hard for credibility. I am willing to accept the likelihood that if we had been more open about why these events had occurred, our support would have held steady and been less tentative.

It was necessary for the company to communicate effectively with the external world—shareholders, the media, Wall Street—in order to establish credibility, but this could only be accomplished by managing communications within the company more thoughtfully and efficiently.

Parkinson demonstrated in his law that as a business

expands, the number of bureaucrats grows, and the number of "messages" exchanged grows twice as fast, since each person must communicate with everyone else. As internal communications swells by 90 percent, the organization ends up by cutting itself off from the very people it is supposed to serve.

This overloading of communications is no less true in other areas. Shareholders, for example, are primarily interested in the value we create for their investment in us. We are not only inexpert, generally, in presenting our accomplishments to them but we feel responsible for counseling them on foreign trade, the vagaries of the U.S. dollar, family finance, technology, global politics, sociology, international law, etc. We should, instead, concentrate on the effective communication of essential information—and, thus, establish the credibility crucial to corporate survival.

EMHART FROM THE INSIDE

The intellectual exercise involved in contributing to this unique book, to think about my own corporate life and to reflect on what I have been doing daily for nearly two decades, has led me to some interesting observations of which the word credibility seemed to be the essence or nucleus.

Looking at my life through that specific prism I find I have been performing a number of relevant functions not generally associated with the chief executive, at least in management literature.

Ask what the chief executive does, and the traditional answer is that he or she "plans, organizes, coordinates and controls." This definition hasn't been really challenged, or changed much since it was first stated some 66 years ago.

I can refine it a bit by describing the roles as being decision maker, planner, economist and strategist. I find that I act as "counselor, arbitrator, philosopher, and worrier."

As counselor, I find I increasingly pull back from the actual decision making, and in a judicial context, hand the day-to-day decisions back to the people who have to implement them.

Implicit in this umpire's role is that of arbitrator, that is, as chief executive, I am the one person whose presence and authority can negotiate major staff differences and develop compatibility among the different needs and ambitions of staff, line employees and shareholders. It's a balancing act, orchestrating the competencies and skills of the various managers and people necessary to the operation of the company.

In the last two of these four roles, the concepts of international and external communications merge. A chief executive, I've found, must be the company's principal *philosophical* leader—a symbol of the personality and character of the business. We have to set the example for tomorrow's executives who will have to be broader persons intellectually than their predecessors. This means that we have to be able to talk and write interestingly, even provocatively, about business (such as arguing that we communicate too much; more on this later). We must be articulate, persuasive advocates for private enterprise, and we must be able to address ourselves to the more subtle psychological meaning of work, of security, of rewards and motivation.

My favorite role, now that I've identified it, is that of the *worrier*. Sounds as if I've been practicing acute paranoia. Not so.

Rather, I am thinking about the creative ability to see problems where no one else does, to identify headaches before they become real—perhaps, most of all, to be the one constant enemy of the status quo. Managers have a predilection for the comfort and security of the familiar. This is the scourge of corporate progress, or growth. "Don't rock the boat" thinking has tipped more corporate canoes than any other managerial malady.

PREPARATION FOR TOMORROW'S MANAGERS

One wit said that the only person capable of handling the vast array of problems of the future chief executive died some 2,000 years ago. Most current chief executives have their own theories as to what constitutes the most effective undergraduate and graduate training program for tomorrow's responsibilities.

Traditionally most business school surveys show liberal arts and business vying for the top spot, with engineering and the sciences fluctuating as the nation's love affair with technology waxes and wanes. Some, because of the increasingly litigious character of the business environment, emphasize law. I confess I'm an ex-lawyer myself, but I majored in sociology in my undergraduate days. Law brings out valuable qualities of analysis, concentration and judgment. But it must be leavened with other insights, because it is essentially a negative business. I would suggest that tomorrow's chief executive should have a solid grasp of world history and of international economics and politics. Since more and more corporations are multinational, the executive must also be multicultural.

I would suggest that he or she dip into the behavioral sciences, not to be a master propagandist but to better understand how and why people form attitudes and opinions, and how they cope with them. Some anthropology would be useful. Much of the curricula at the schools of diplomacy, such as The Fletcher School of Law and Diplomacy, Tufts University, appears tailor-made for an international chief executive's preparation, and I commend these schools to any with such ambitions.

But it matters little what the scope and breadth of the education is if executives lose their curiosity about the world, let their intellectual interests atrophy, retreat behind the balance sheets and the potted palms of their executive sanctuary, and limit their reading to the prescribed journals, papers and periodicals of their trade. A wag once said it's hard to look up to a leader who keeps his ear to the ground. To be sure, one of the important skills that each of, or a combination of, these disciplines teaches the aspiring executive is the ability to deal effectively with information, both that coming in and that going out.

CREDIBILITY AND COMMUNICATIONS

It is widely assumed that the remarkable developments in communications technologies automatically improve communications. It would indeed be wonderful if this were true, but unfortunately, in the real world of the exchange of ideas, information and opinions, this is emphatically not the case.

There are both statistical as well as psychological validations for this opinion.

For example, the amount of information directed to the public is growing enormously. Television is ubiquitous, reaching about 98 percent of all the people in the United States. That's more people than have telephones—or indoor plumbing.

More books were published last year than ever before—about 50,000—and bookstores are growing at the rate of 10 percent a year. The number of magazines published is at a record high. In fact, the media are growing at twice the rate of the GDP.

But studies show that per capita consumption of words is down to an anemic 1.2 percent growth rate a year. This means that people see and hear less and less of the torrents of information beamed at them.

The late Marshal McLuhan characterized this as a process of "perceptual numbing," a sort of psychological Novocain through which we have increased our threshold to all types of perceptions to such a high level that almost all communications fall short.

I am concerned about the effectiveness of our communications. Sometimes I feel that we behave like lottery winners squandering our riches—throwing words about wildly in the hope that they will take effect somewhere.

I grew up in an era where clarity of communications was an absolute must. But today, we live in a world where communications are so pervasive that we seem to be debasing communications and cheapening the intrinsic value of our language by indiscriminate overuse. One might even properly ask: "What's left to communicate?"

Furthermore, the proliferating information and communication technologies cut two ways; therein lies the dilemma. More information can clarify an issue but, paradoxically, it can also obscure and complicate. It can bring groups together, and it can help groups to splinter. It can bring fresh ideas to the marketplace and more thoughts and opinions, as well as general information, to the public—our shareholders, employees or our neighbors in the communities in which we live or work. But it does so at the cost of raising the noise level to the point where nothing can clearly be heard or seen.

As we create, produce and process all this information—ostensibly to reduce uncertainty and give us a basis for controlling events, our lives and our future—we often are, instead, breeding uncertainty. Because we don't really know enough to comprehend the consequences of what this information reveals, we are often led to a feeling that things are getting out of control.

As business leaders, we are buried deeper and deeper in overloads of information, information-about-information and, to use the new buzz word, "misinformation." We are told that this cornucopia of communications will make it easier for us to arrive at informed decisions which, presumably, will enable us to "get things under control."

It is a byproduct of the American culture to assume, grandly, and without qualification, that "too much is always better than not enough."

Is it not possible that we could be overinformed? As a chief executive, I can assure you I don't really need half of the data "someone" thinks I'm anxiously awaiting.

Let me ask you this:

As we embrace more and more technology to create and disseminate more and more information simultaneously to more and more people, are we not in danger of losing our bearings? Have we anything truly worthwhile to say? And what about our credibility?

I am in no sense advocating that we burn the books and cut the radio and TV wires. I am not suggesting that ignorance is bliss.

What I am trying to bring forth is that we need to back away from our traditional preoccupation with the trappings of communications—the hardware, which has taken on a deity of its own—and take a fresh, objective look at what and why we are communicating.

As I look about in society, I see increasing evidence that we are beginning to mature and understand that "more is not always better." For example, although we can replace practically all the major parts of our bodies through surgery, and our skills have become almost godlike, we now seek second and third opinions before committing to an operation. Shouldn't we apply the same restraint and comparable analytical discipline to our communications?

When we are sensitive to the credibility achieved through effective communications, we tend to look more critically at a number of the enduring myths regularly communicated by many of my contemporaries. Let's take profit, probably the most misused, overused six-letter word in the lexicon of executives.

Most of us are fairly convinced that it is the economic illiteracy of the public that creates the hostility between society and business and, of course, that threatens the free enterprise system itself. So, doggedly, we insist on "educating" them. The litany about the meaning of profits goes on and on—boring most, convincing few (and adding little luster to our credibility).

It is here, in this dialogue, that business leaders can show some innovative communications leadership, I believe.

I've always felt that the unnatural comparisons we're obliged to report publicly between one quarter and the same quarter a year ago do not really tell our shareholders or employees all that has happened, or why. Net earnings are certainly a tangible measure, but they're the past—not necessarily the future. What does have meaning, historically, are the investments in research, in technology, in new plants and equipment. And, in our case, investments in acquisitions. So, we tend to emphasize these, rather than bugling the profits (even though we've had four consecutive record years).

The freshest and most relevant idea along these lines I've read about during my business career comes appropriately from Peter Drucker, who is certainly one of the most thoughtful and prolific writers on business and management. Drucker suggests that businessmen owe it to themselves and to society to hammer home the point that there is no such thing as "profit." There are only "costs." Costs of doing business and costs of staying in business, costs of labor and raw materials, costs of capital, as well as the costs of today's jobs and costs of tomorrow's jobs and tomorrow's pensions.

From this perspective, it is not the business that earns a profit adequate to its genuine costs of capital, or to the risks of tomorrow and the needs of tomorrow's workers and pensioners, that "rips off society." It is the business that fails to do so.

This point of view offers considerable opportunity to develop an affirmative—and more credible—appreciation and understanding of profit than the conventional wisdom as preached in the typical economic education program.

Intuitively, I know that more information, more communications, does not increase the quality of the process—but it surely comforts us that we "are getting the word out."

As we increase the decibel level and pile on the material, I believe we wear out our welcome, erode our credibility—and outrageously deceive ourselves that we are truly communicating.

Paul F. Oreffice

Paul F. Oreffice is president and chief executive officer of the Dow Chemical Company and chairman of the executive committee, positions he has held since May 3, 1978.

A Dow employee since 1953, Mr. Oreffice began his Dow career in Midland, Michigan, then moved to successive international assignments in Switzerland, Italy, Brazil and Spain before becoming in 1966 the first president of Dow Chemical Latin America in Coral Gables, Florida. In 1970, he returned to Midland as financial vice-president of the company, a position he held until being named president of Dow Chemical U.S.A. in August 1975. He was elected to the Dow board of directors in 1971.

Mr. Oreffice is currently a director of Dow Corning Corporation, CIGNA Corporation, Northern Telecom Limited and Comerica Bank-Midland. He is on the Policy Committee of The Business Roundtable and on the boards of trustees of American Enterprise Institute, the Conference Board and the Midland Community Center.

A native of Venice, Italy, Mr. Oreffice first came to the United States with his family when he was 12 years old. He later became a citizen and served in the U.S. Army during the Korean conflict. A 1949 graduate of Purdue University with a B.S. degree in chemical engineering, he received an honorary doctor of engineering degree from Purdue in 1976. He also holds honorary doctoral degrees in industrial management from Lawrence Institute of Technology, science from Saginaw Valley State College and business administration from Tri-State University and South Dakota School of Mines and

Technology. He is on the board of governors of the Purdue University Foundation. In 1982, Oreffice received the Sagamore of the Wabash Award—Indiana's highest honor—for his service to education.

In 1966, Oreffice received the Encomienda del Merito Civil (Order of Civil Merit) from the government of Spain, and, in 1978, the Italian government honored him with the title of "Grand Ufficiale." In 1981, he was awarded the International Palladium Medal by the Société de Chimie Industrielle. In 1983, he was awarded the Chemical Industry Medal by the Society of Chemical Industry. He is the first person to receive both the Palladium Medal and the Chemical Industry Medal.

9
PEOPLE SELECTION—
THE RIGHT PERSON
MAKES THE DIFFERENCE

By Paul F. Oreffice
President and Chief Executive Officer
The Dow Chemical Company

Often I am referred to by people within the company as the phantom personnel director. It's a nickname that I view seriously and with some affection. But the nickname underscores what I consider to be one of the most important responsibilities I have as chief executive officer of Dow Chemical Company. That responsibility is ensuring that we have the right people in the right job at the right time.

People selection and people placement have become such critical elements for business today because without proper selection and placement it is impossible to maximize the skills people can bring to their jobs. These are critical times when employee skills must be tapped for the present and future economic success of any organization.

Within The Dow Chemical Company, we have both formal and informal methods for selecting people for various job openings. The formal process is one in which the managers of each of our geographic areas conduct annual reviews of the people within their areas to assess not only their on-the-job performance, but also their potential for assuming greater responsibility in the near term. Then, annually, the presidents of our six geographic areas and I, along with other key staff members, spend five full days reviewing approximately 1,000 people who have been identified by various managers. This annual review is an attempt to do a broad brush assessment of our people-resource strengths on a global basis.

In addition to this formal review, each month our salary committee, composed of key management members of our board of directors and officers of the company, meets to talk about people and to review again the people resources in various functions within the company. For example, one month we might have the vice-president for research and development in to review not only some of the research activities but also some of the accomplishments of people within the research function and to receive from that manager recommendations relative to the future deployment of those people into other functions in the company. As part of this formalized review process we also expect our employee relations department and its key people really to know our people resources throughout the company both on a geographical basis for each of our six operating areas and on a global basis.

The typical process of filling a key job within the Dow system begins with drawing up a "long list" of candidates that we think are suited for that job. We consider them regardless of whether or not they are ready for a geographical move, regardless of whether they have been on their current job for too short of a period of time and therefore should not be moved, or whether they are performing so well that it would be difficult to replace them. Then we start weeding them out. From the long list we wind up with a short list of perhaps three or four people who are prime candidates for the job assignment. Any one of those three or four could fill the job. Finally, the individual who is best for this job, not only from the standpoint of the company's needs, but also from that of the individual's career development, is selected.

Determining which should take priority—company interest or employee development—is not often an easy task. But within Dow, more times than not, what is in the best interest of the employee's development is considered equally with the company needs. In many cases we put the interest of employee development ahead of the interest of the company. We do this because every job can be approached in a different way. If we merely create an organizational chart and within that chart spell out the major functions of the job, we lose what we consider to be a very valuable commodity—flexibility and management style in the approach to that job.

For example, if a manager has an opening and looks for a candidate to fill that slot, he or she may feel that the job can entail only the five or six key responsibilities possessed by the person who currently holds the job. We think this approach limits the potential creativity that could result by looking at people from other areas who have the basic skills sought, but who also can bring with them a fresh approach to the implementation of some of the basic responsibilities of the job.

Within Dow we call this "job enlargement" or the "whole job concept." Introduced by former chairman of the board Earle Barnes, in the early 1970s, the whole-job concept has been expanded over the years and I'm a great fan of it. For example, when I was appointed financial vice-president of The Dow Chemical Company, I had reporting to me the controller, the treasurer, the industrial relations and pension fund management personnel. When I left that post to become president of Dow U.S.A., the largest of our six geographical areas, the new financial vice-president did not have the extensive background necessary to oversee the controllers department. On the other hand, he thoroughly understood the legal and tax areas, so we added the legal and tax departments to the financial vice-president's post and transferred the reporting function of the controller elsewhere. Then, when this individual was replaced, we changed the financial vice-president's post once again, molding it to fit that individual. Not only in this job, but also in many jobs within Dow, we attempt to mold the talent of the person to the position he or she is filling.

When we go outside of a narrow functional line to select a manager who doesn't have direct background experience in that new function, there may be some questions as to expertise. Occasionally some expertise is lost, but it will be restored through the practice of what we call in Dow "cross-functional fertilization." We may take some individuals out of the research area, for instance, and place them in a marketing function where they can easily visualize how the products they discovered and developed are received in the marketplace. Then, after a while, we bring them back into the research function where they can apply the marketing knowledge they have gained to their R&D objectives. Functional cross-fertilization helps tie together the three key functions of The Dow Chemical Company as well as its six geographical areas. The three company functions are manufacturing, marketing, and research and development activities, as these take place in each of our geographic regions around the world.

In selecting people for promotion or new job assignments there is always the risk that a mistake may be made, and that the person who has been appointed may not meet expectations. When this occurs, the mistake should be corrected—but in a positive manner. A company will not be successful without taking risks, not only in commercial ventures and in marketing, but also in promoting employees.

One lesson we've learned in Dow as we practice the whole-job concept and cross-functional fertilization is that the potential for failure is greater when an individual is asked to make a double move. This can occur when we take someone who is very good in a function in one region—for example, in research within the United States—and place him or her in both a different function and a different geographical environment. In many cases we've found that this is just not a productive use of people. The cultural and the functional differences are too great to handle all at once.

Because Dow has practiced cross-functional fertilization for more than 20 years, it has been successful at eliminating the potential for resentment that exists when a manager is brought into an organization without having been a product of that infrastructure. For example, when I became the financial vice-president of the company, I had never had any direct experience in finance—and this was the only financial job I've ever had within Dow. (I'm a chemical engineer by training and I came up from marketing.) Since I came into the financial function with no formal financial experience within the company, I was a classic target for resentment. But I think what really counts is the individual's performance. If you come in and show that you can do the job, you are accepted, regardless of the years of background that you might have had.

Aside from the skills an individual may bring to the job, I think one of the key elements of a successful manager is that person's ability to motivate people to get things done. Getting people to work as a team so that they are all pulling in one direction rather than as 10 or 15 individuals all going in their own way and seeking to accomplish their own agenda is of critical importance to the success of any organization.

Dow has a reputation of being a very lean organization, and we're quite proud of that. In fact, our corporate staff, including all of our secretarial support and others, numbers less than 250 people out of more than 50,000 employees worldwide. We don't have official company organizational charts. In fact, we discourage the development of formalized organizational charts because they tend to put people into boxes and to restrict not only their creative approach to the job but also their flexibility to react to a changing business environment. Since we advocate minimum bureaucracy within Dow, we have very few levels of management. People know what's expected of them and know that they're expected to seize opportunities, maximize them wherever possible and minimize potential problems. I'm a firm believer that the *fewer levels you have, the better off you are.* In fact, the ability to move is inversely proportional to the number of levels of management within the company. In companies with many management levels, you have to ask the question, "What are those resources doing? Are they being creative? Are they being productive? Or are they merely sitting around, not really being motivated and merely attempting to justify their existence, or meddling too much in other people's business and creating more work for them in the process?" I truly believe it pays to be a lean organization.

Dow also advocates developing its managers from within. I'm very much a believer in the school of thought that an individual learns more by doing than by looking over somebody's shoulder in a management seminar or reading case studies. In my opinion, learning by doing and on-the-job training have been highly successful for Dow. We also believe that an individual need not have a degree from a particular school in order to succeed in Dow. In fact, Dow is probably looser in this concept than many others. For example, an M.B.A. isn't required for an individual working in finance, although the degree may be of benefit to that person. It works better, we have found, to mold a person's ability to the job rather than the job to the person.

Although people selection is a critical skill managers must develop in their approach to management responsibilities, there is another critical area that requires not only delicacy but also a great deal of empathy on the part of managers toward their subordinates. I'm referring to the proper way of handling a situation when an employee perceives either rightly or wrongly that he or she has failed in something. The manager's motivational task is even tougher when workers set such high standards of performance for themselves that they are not satisfied with their performance. Communication is probably the only way that a manager can effectively monitor an individual's performance.

I stress the importance of communication because it entails not only day-to-day interface with staff members but also review of their written and progress reports. If there is effective two-way communication, a manager can detect poor performance before it becomes a significant problem for the employee. When this potentially "demotivating" situation is detected, the best thing a manager can do is to review with the employee why he or she may not have done as well as expected, discuss the perceptions others may have about the employee's job performance and suggest how the employee can improve. Talking it out is the proper course. Obviously, how a manager approaches each individual requires recognition of that individual's sensitivities and the manager's own assessment of the situation.

Usually, a demotivated or frustrated person is really an individual who hasn't accomplished very much in the job. Let me give you another example. Very often it isn't the job you're given but what you do with that job. Two people can approach the same job in an entirely different manner and, depending on the employee, the job will vary in importance to the company. For example, when I was sent to Brazil as a one-man operation to start a marketing company, I realized I had two choices. I could develop a nice little sales company where I could do all right or I could try to make things happen. Obviously, I took the second choice and within three years Dow Brazil was the second largest chemical company in Brazil—and we didn't even have a single manufacturing plant there. I created the job and developed it into a major function within the company. The job name didn't change, but it was a completely different job when I left than it had been prior to my going there.

In the case of a demotivated or frustrated employee, the decision may be to replace the poor performer. The manager may then have the managerial problem of convincing the new employee that the decision to accept the assignment is a good one, despite other perceptions. It's very important to communicate to the new person going into the job that the very reason for putting him or her there is because that person has the skills to revitalize the function. The manager must be able to communicate well in order to help the new employee realize that he or she is bringing to that function the critical skills needed to help the organization realize its potential.

A manager of people comes across all types of individuals in the organizaaion, ranging from the individual who is content to do only what is asked to the individual who is highly ambitious, highly motivated and even steps on people's toes to reach certain goals. Sometimes it takes a while to discover or recognize those who may be using others to climb the corporate ladder, but, eventually, the manager who communicates well finds out.

I've made almost a personal credo for the last 15 to 20 years an innate suspicion of anybody who is too smooth. I always do a double-take when someone impresses me immediately because I want to make sure that I don't just like the exterior. I want to have confidence in what's behind the exterior, and I want to be sure that that person really has the business skills he or she claims to have.

Another skill I look for in the selection of managers is the ability of a person to stand up and take the heat for a decision he or she believes is the correct decision for the future, even though it is controversial at the moment. The strong manager will realize that the controversial decision will prove in time to be beneficial for the organization and that confidence comes with decision making. I like people who come in and say, "We have a problem. This is what we can do about it. What do you think?" Probably in 95 percent of the cases the decision they suggest is the right one and I simply agree with them. It is important that they have identified a problem, determined the proper ways to address it and begun to implement the solutions. In 5 percent of cases, however, managers should work with others to solve them. In these cases, it seems, one brain can never be better than two or more.

Ambitious managers, managers who are willing to take risks, are accustomed to job growth and advancement. Within Dow we have a very interesting program to help create openings in the top management of the company and to ensure that we have a continuous supply of fresh blood in the management ranks of the organization. We call this program "deceleration." The basic philosophy of our deceleration policy is to create opportunities for younger managers by making room at the top for them. We came to the conclusion that after a number of years at the top levels of management, where the pressures are great, people can get worn out. Thus, we decided to advance the time frame at which managers leave their executive positions, and yet leave open the possibility of using the talents of those top managers who still wish to contribute to the company.

We created the program we refer to as "deceleration" in response to this need. Deceleration describes the process of going from working 110 percent of the time and shifting toward a gradual phase-out toward retirement. When executives enter the first year of deceleration, they give up their line management responsibilities and devote approximately 80 percent of their time to the company, possibly 70 percent the following year, and 60 percent the year after that, until eventually they retire completely from the board and the company. Top managers in the deceleration program have a tremendous value to the company in that the expertise they have developed over the years can be shared with the current management. Yet, they really are in no one's hip pocket. They are independent managerial consultants to the line management of the company. They know the company inside out, and sometimes they're able to offer a perspective that is not jaded by the pressures of the hectic day-to-day business environment.

Another key area of management is the ability to recognize when a job is becoming too big for one person to handle. The proper response when this occurs is to delegate authority. Through delegation of authority, managers demonstrate their approach to the job by their action versus their words. How much they are willing to delegate is a further indication of their confidence or comfort level in their job assignment. When a manager lets subordinates do a job and sees that they can get things accomplished well, then the manager can relax and get on to the broader objective of strategy planning, which is an essential part of his or her management function.

Good managers use delegation of authority to promote and expose their staffs, as well as give them other experiences. Sometimes, when authority is delegated, a manager may take credit for the idea or program that a subordinate has developed. But if a manager takes credit for something that another has done, that subordinate will be benefited because, in the long-run, the manager who took the credit will always know in the back of his mind whose idea it really was.

Whether or not a manager delegates authority to staff is easy to recognize. One of the things that I notice when I visit various functions of the company throughout the United States or around the world is how members of a manager's staff act in my presence and the manager's. If they are free and open in their discussions of business, even sometimes poking fun at the manager, I know there's been good communication, good support on the part of the manager for staff and the development of teamwork and the concept that everyone in the organization is working for the common good.

I've dwelt a great deal on the management responsibilities of people selection, delegation of authority and the necessity of recognizing that there's an appropriate time to step aside and make way for the next generation of managers in the organization. But there is yet another important aspect of the successful manager—the ability to combine their job and family life. A good manager finds time for both. I meet with a lot of our new employees, and a question they often ask is, "Can you have fun on the job?" or "Is management all work and no play?" My answer always is that if you're not having fun on your job, you ought to try something else. If you're not having fun, if you're not motivated, stimulated and challenged, if you don't feel excited about your job, then you're not going to be good for yourself or for the company.

I also tell young people, especially young managers who seek advice on how to succeed, that, in matters of the job or the family, everything is important but, in my opinion, the family comes first. That's why I'm not enthusiastic about workaholics. I think a manager has to lead a balanced life—job, family and charitable community activities all help to make a complete person. The successful manager shouldn't have to work 12 hours every day. Rather, I think he or she might have a very normal eight-hour day two or three days in a row and then have to work 16 hours a day for a couple of days because a particular business situation requires that type of intense concentration and dedication to the job. One of the things that irritates me most is the stereotype on television of a manager who disregards home and family completely and rises to the top, climbing over everyone in the process while ignoring any responsibility to the community. More typical, I believe, is the happily married manager who combines home and family successfully to the advantage of both. In my opinion, a happy home life helps to provide a stable climate for the manager and permits him or her to direct attention to the job 100 percent when on the job.

Some people might say, "You may put in only eight or nine hours in the office but then you take home a full briefcase every night." To the young manager I would say, "I think I'm better off taking a briefcase home, having dinner with my family, spending some time with my children and then attacking my briefcase full of work while I'm at home with my wife." I think that is more productive time for me than spending excessive time at the office.

Some young managers have asked me if it's wise for them to socialize off the job with the people who work for them or if they should only socialize with their peers. I think that balance is necessary on the job, but it is also necessary off the job. I absolutely believe that it's proper for managers to socialize with a cross-section of people they interact with on the job. In my case, I think I hear what's going on in the rumor mill more frequently in the cafeteria or at the local tennis center than I do on the job. It's important to be a part of the organization, both the formal organization on the job and the informal infrastructure in the community, to really know what's happening in the organization and to practice communication skills as a manager.

There is and must be room for ethics in business. I believe that there is no difference between moral and business ethics—they are the same. And if you don't have good, ethical practices, you're not going to succeed, whether on the job, in your community life, or in your home life. Some people may perceive that the good of society is more important than profit, but I feel that profit is the way in which we in business can support good causes. If we are profitable, not only can we produce products and services that people need and provide meaningful jobs and income for our workers but we also have the ability as a result of our profitable operations to support many of the community, educational and charitable objectives of our environment. All in all, business and moral ethics, in my mind, are completely intertwined.

So, as we've looked at some of the management skills and some of the critical decisions that need to be considered when selecting a manager for a particular job, I think we also need to review some of the qualities or characteristics that the so-called ideal manager should possess. As I said earlier, I think the best manager is the manager who knows how to make other people work toward the common objective. That is what the manager stands for—how to manage the energy and overcome the inertia of an organization to reach its identified goals. Managing your resources, people, financial assets and raw materials, is another part of management. It may appear that managing resources is easier than managing people but, if you manage people well and properly delegate authority to your people, you will have managed your resources well at the same time.

Learning how to delegate is of tremendous importance to the manager. And if you don't get used to making decisions, it will soon be very hard for you to make them. Good managers also will allow their staffs to make mistakes but will not allow them to make repetitive mistakes. There's nothing wrong with making mistakes. In fact, Ben Branch, former president of Dow Chemical, used to say that he made more mistakes than anybody in the history of the company. It's inevitable that those who take risks will make mistakes. The only crime is to make the same mistake over and over again. If we don't learn from mistakes, then we have failed. Good managers also give credit to those who deserve it. Finally, a good manager is an individual who has developed the ability and the self-confidence to take appropriate risks.

Today in business too many managers get into a posture

where they become comfortable and reason, "Why take a risk?" But I believe if you don't take a risk, you'll never build anything, you'll never excel, you'll never surpass your competition. Determining the appropriate risk and taking that risk at the appropriate time is a critical skill a top manager needs to develop. It can be sharpened and finely honed through previous business experiences and communications on the job.

Finally, there is one other element that needs exploration—crisis management. Many times people in management overreact to the nature of a crisis. A good manager in a business crisis is a person who knows how to keep a level head, keep the perspective of the company foremost and not let his or her emotions run wild. When a crisis situation occurs, a manager should seek out the brightest people available, elicit their opinions on the situation, get together all the data possible and then take charge of a course of action through which the organization can attack that crisis.

As we know, business crises today take on a variety of forms. Positive crisis situations in which a decision has to be made quickly on the potential acquisition of a company or product line can present tremendous business opportunities for the organization. But there are also more negative types of crises, such as a public image crisis or a long-term economic crisis, in which the organization falls upon bad economic times either through its own mismanagement or through the broader, external economic pressures on the organization.

Let me dwell a bit upon the business crisis in which a company may be involved in a severe downturn of business of lasting duration—perhaps two or three years. Such a downturn could result in all kinds of drains being placed on the resources of the organization, preventing it from building or expanding into new operations, preventing proper reward of its people, not having adequate resources to do the research it wants to do, and so on. A good manager is one that doesn't let the crisis go on for too long before starting to take some measures to prevent a large impact on the business. The more anticipation there is, the better able the company will be to weather economic downturns or other crises.

How you prepare for such a stormy weather period or how you batten down the hatches requires good perceptive skills.

When you start seeing some of the early warning signs, you decide at that point not to add as many resources as you normally would, whether it's capital resources or people. The objective should be not to increase the liabilities more than necessary as a way to keep the sails trimmed as you plot a course through the rough waters of the economic environment. Sometimes in a crisis the manager will have to pull in all the reins, draw back the delegation of authority and give more directives than he or she normally would give in a calmer business environment. This type of centralized management practice is necessary because it is critical at this juncture for everyone to pull the same way. If you have five managers who begin to tighten their belts and another who goes merrily along his own way, not only will you have internal dissension within the organization but you'll have another leak in the ship that will only result in faster bailing later. When everybody knows that everybody across the board is working to minimize the impact of the economic downturn on the organization, then morale among all employees will be uniform and will be easier to maintain. Once the crisis has been weathered, the very critical time occurs when the manager has to be perceptive enough to begin loosening the reins and delegating more responsibility and authority down the line.

Determining the proper person for the job is a key management task. So too, are good communication skills in a crisis situation. It's extremely important to get everybody to pull in the same direction, to understand the challenges facing the organization and to motivate people to work as a team to tackle the problem. Communication skills are probably more necessary at this point than any other skills.

In the final analysis, the skills necessary for a person to be a good manager can all be summed up in the exercise of good judgment tempered with common sense. In reality, common sense can dictate the proper managerial course of action—whether it be in selecting the right person for the right job, delegating authority where necessary, recognizing the limitations inherent in any one person's individual capabilities and selecting the right path for an organization in a business crisis. Through on-the-job experience and the learning that occurs by taking appropriate business risks, good managers will call upon common sense to help them exercise good judgment. By using common sense, these managers will help the company or organization grow and prosper—and they will fulfill their management responsibilities.

Jerome M. Rosow

Jerome M. Rosow, president and founder of Work in America Institute, Inc., has had careers in both government and industry devoted to manpower, employee relations and public affairs. He served as manager of employee relations at ESSO Europe, and then as public affairs manager, Exxon Corporation, New York. His government service includes: assistant secretary of labor 1969-71 and chairman of the President's Advisory Committee on Federal Pay (1971-84). Mr. Rosow was president of the Industrial Relations Research Association for 1979. Currently, he is an advisor to the Committee for Economic Development and a member of the United States Business and Advisory Committee of the OECD, Paris.

In 1974, Mr. Rosow edited *The Worker and the Job: Coping with Change* (Prentice-Hall) as chairman of The American Assembly on "The Changing World of Work." He was co-editor with Clark Kerr of *Work in America: The Decade Ahead* (Van Nostrand Reinhold) in June 1979; editor of *Productivity: Prospects for Growth* (Van Nostrand Reinhold) in 1981; and author of *Made in America* (Facts On File) in 1984. He has contributed numerous articles to such publications as *The Harvard Business Review* and the *Advanced Management Journal*.

In November 1980, Mr. Rosow received the U.S. Comptroller General's Public Service Award.

10
SUMMING UP THE
VIEWS FROM THE TOP

By Jerome M. Rosow
President
Work in America Institute

When we began work on this book almost two years ago, it was with the idea that the time was right for a book on management by those who stand at the pinnacle of American business and industry. We believed that such a work, based on each CEO's personal experiences, would offer new insights about big business in the '80s and would, in fact, comprise an historical document. We invited each of the CEOs to speak for himself and for his company—to speak for business in general—and to speak in concert with a group of peers. Each author was given carte blanche to write about those management issues that were most meaningful both to him and to the company he heads, in the context of how big business is establishing a foundation for the future. Thus, when they were completed, these views from the top addressed not only the current status of the enterprises over which the contributors hold critical stewardship but also of the long-term growth and continuity of these enterprises. Each contributor took note not only of the state of his respective corporation but also of the state of the society and the economy. Interestingly, a commonality of important themes emerged.

Although each chapter stands alone as the personal testament of an individual heading an organization with a unique history and culture, several of them delve in depth into the same or similar issues. Not every one, of course, is concerned with every issue, but time and again, in two or three or four separate accounts, similar areas of action crop up. We found that at least eight themes threaded their way through the entire book, rating extensive treatment by some CEOs or brief mention by others.

They were:

- Reshaping the organization
- Defining a strategic plan
- Growth and response to change
- Motivation and managing people
- Decision making
- Encouraging entrepreneurship
- Developing executives for the next generation
- Creating a corporate culture

This overview of all nine chapters was planned as a guide to assist the reader in identifying the predominant themes. It highlights portions of each of the chapters and clarifies the interrelationships of ideas. At the same time, it makes clear that styles of leadership vary widely and that there are marked individual differences among CEOs, as indicated by the emphasis they place on particular themes.

RESHAPING THE ORGANIZATION

The organization is a dynamic arrangement of functions, services, products, people and physical assets to achieve corporate goals on a continuing basis.

The CEO has both the power and the responsibility to determine whether the organization as a management concept is compatible with the needs of the business in the long term or whether reorganization is needed.

Most of the CEOs in this book have refused to look at the organization as an immutable, permanent form. Both failures and successes have triggered complete and thorough organizational shakeups to reshape and reorganize corporate relationships. In other organizations, hierarchical, top-heavy empires of the past—and present—have given way to flatter, more streamlined organizations.

Reorganization is always a painful process and one which most managers and employers tend to resist. It requires a vision of the future of the business, derived from an intimate knowledge of the existing resources—and a CEO who is ready to take major risks in order to disconnect from the past and carry the corporation forward into uncharted territory.

Edward Telling's chapter about Sears is an insider's view of the transformation of one of the nation's greatest retailers into an integrated but broadly diversified retail service organization. Telling describes the task he undertook in 1978 with a company that had become ingrown, set in its ways and lacking in competitive momentum. This is a revealing and exciting story of the actions taken by the CEO to regenerate the corporation by changing its structure; facing up to a new competitive environment; dealing with the board of directors; infusing new, younger leadership; installing a strong planning process; and undertaking a far-reaching diversification into consumer financial services.

The turnaround of stick-in-the-mud Sears would have been impossible unless critical measures to reduce the layers of a tradition-bound, top-heavy management had been taken by Telling and his associates.

Charles Brown took office as CEO of the giant AT&T in 1979 and was immediately confronted with the most fundamental challenge to the company's future—the virtual breakup of the system. This traumatic shock to the corporation and its million employees, as well as to the nation, tested the mettle and the talents of Brown in a way that no other CEO had ever been tested. His chapter is a classic description of how he managed the radical reshaping of the nation's telecommunications structure. He examines first the forces which led to the far-reaching decision to dismantle a monopoly that was an integral part of the nation's social and economic fabric.

Reorganization of the company affectionately known as "Ma Bell" required government approval—but it also required a complex planning process unprecedented in corporate history. The painful fact was that this unwanted task ironically required the same dedication, assurance and energy as the task of building Bell. How could executives and managers join a wrecking crew to tear down this national institution, heralded as the most efficient in the world, create in its place a new structure, modern, flexible and strong enough to fill the vacuum, and enter an entirely new era of industrial competition all at the same time?

As the operation unfolded step by step and options were considered, reorganization emerged as the best solution to minimize the impact of divestiture. Six main components became obsolete overnight, with AT&T losing three-quarters of its assets—almost $100 billion—and nearly two-thirds of its employees. Simultaneously, the headquarters staff was cut to less than one-tenth of its size in the old AT&T, through managerial and professional personnel transfers, retirements and separations.

At the same time, this stripped-down corporation was thrown directly into a new world of stiff competition at all levels: long distance, home telephones, office-communications systems and switching and transmission equipment.

Brown describes the new organization and explains how it is positioned to meet the future with flexibility, responsiveness, accountability and market focus. Then he reveals the new model of AT&T as a multinational enterprise, viable overseas and returning to markets abandoned half a century ago.

The concept of streamlining a nonbureaucratic organization is described clearly in Oreffice's chapter on Dow Chemical. As a lean organization, Dow has fewer than 250 employees, including all secretarial and support staff, in the world headquarters of a corporation with more than 50,000 employees worldwide. There are no official organization charts because Oreffice believes that charts restrict people's creative approach to the job. Instead, Oreffice stresses flexibility and the capacity to react to a changing business environment. He feels strongly that the organization's ability to move is inversely proportional to the numbers of levels of management within the company. Thus, he recommends that the number of levels be held to a minimum and that managers be given the freedom to seize opportunities and maximize their own achievements.

Wendt of SmithKline Beckman takes an Olympian view of the late twentieth-century multinational corporation, approaching the role of the CEO within the context of the corporation, and the role of the organization within the broader framework of the total world society. To operate as a fully integrated organization, "where each of the parts supports some vital role of the other parts," the corporation must be "organic," not mechanical, says Wendt. Quoting Robert Eccles of Harvard University, he points out that the corporation must emphasize "informality and networks of authority based on expertise rather than hierarchy and high levels of stress and ambiguity." This organic perspective rejects the prospect of diversification through acquisitions or the development of business unrelated to the company's major business.

Wendt reflects a viewpoint similar to that of Oreffice in Dow, proposing fewer management levels, more participation, a hands-on approach to business and more delegation to small teams. He advocates decreasing the importance of middle management and compressing the organizational hierarchy into a newly evolving model of the flat organization. This is a model that demands less formality, fewer levels of review and a collapse of the highly structured organization (which resembles nothing so much as a multi-tiered wedding cake) into a few tightly packed layers. Flat, he believes, is synonymous with responsiveness and effectiveness.

DEFINING A STRATEGIC PLAN

Strategic planning lies at the heart of the CEO's role. The view from the top of the corporation places the CEO in the catbird seat, from which he is afforded the opportunity of broader vision. His horizons are limited only by his imagination.

In this critical role the CEO must have—or develop—an

understanding of the central core of the enterprise and its goals, which are linked to the world economy, the society and its values, the work force and the marketplace of products and ideas. As strategic planner, the CEO engages his wisdom and that of his associates in a quest for the long-term growth and survival of the enterprise.

Thus, the CEO is essentially a futurist, one who can build on the past successes of the corporation without becoming mired down in old scenarios. The CEO develops strategies to engage the total corporate resources—capital, research and development, personnel and physical assets—to position the company in an effective role for the next decade, or even the next generation. The task is Herculean and the effort must be sustained and timed right if it is to prevail.

The divestiture of AT&T required the ultimate in strategic planning. Brown dissects the issues which created this crisis in corporate survival and reveals the strategy AT&T undertook to preserve its viability as a corporation. Technological advances had set the stage for public policy to deregulate and open competition: microwave radio transmission eliminated the need to procure extensive rights of way and costly aerial or buried cable for long-distance services, overcoming barriers of space, time and money.

In addition, the evolution of solid-state electronics, with the invention of the transistor in the Bell Labs in 1947, gave rise to communications satellites—microwave systems in the sky. These were also the foundation for the explosive growth of the computer industry. In fact, solid-state electronics blurred the distinction between computers and communications. Fearful of change, AT&T resisted the upsetting of the delicate rate structure balance between local and long-distance rates, which pointed to higher prices and less convenience.

At the same time, a 1956 Consent Decree confined the Bell System to its regulated telecommunications market. This massive one-way restructuring placed communications services and computer/data processing out of bounds. The fastest growing and most tempting business was off-limits, unless the monopoly ended.

The necessity of preserving its position in a rapidly changing environment determined AT&T's strategy—settlement of the antitrust issue by negotiating a compromise. First, the marketplace was key; second, the Bell System was perceived as too big, too powerful and too pervasive; third, time was running out and the opportunities of the future were racing by. The result was an agreement to divest—achieving a coherent solution to get AT&T out of the courtroom and back to its own business, including the strange and unsettling agenda of divestiture, reorganization and competition.

The dramatic story of the new Westinghouse, as related by Danforth, was a far-reaching response to the OPEC oil price hike in 1973, when the entire price structure of the energy business skyrocketed. This reversal in utility growth led to four key shifts in strategy:

- Shifting from the manufacture of utility equipment to services for utility customers
- Capitalizing on advanced technology and engineering systems in manufacturing
- Emphasizing high-growth, high-margin businesses, e.g., cable and robotics
- Developing a corporate-wide commitment to quality and productivity

Building upon its reputation, its marketing know-how and its financial muscle, Sears, under Telling's leadership, set out to pursue a strategy of growth and acquisitions in consumer financial services. Four basic principles guided them. They had to be:

- Consumer-oriented businesses, since Sears is fundamentally a merchandiser
- Businesses in which the Sears image of trust made a competitive difference
- National in scope to take advantage of the more than 800 stores coast to coast
- Able to allow Sears to provide greater value to the customers

Assets beyond compare—26 million active credit card accounts, billing $11 billion a year, and 40 million customers—were in place. In 1981, Telling took the first bold, carefully calculated steps in his growth strategy; the acquisition of Dean Witter, the fifth largest national securities firm, and Coldwell Banker, the nation's largest full-service real estate brokerage firm. The in-store distribution channel has proved to be a convenient, easy access, central source for consumer goods and consumer financial services within a high-quality setting.

Management and organization were streamlined. A cross-functional strategic planning committee of senior management was created to reconcile conflict and achieve consensus on the goal of diversification. Telling also achieved a sense of ownership of the strategic business plan by senior management, thus encouraging teamwork.

Expanding its share of the market at Philip Morris, according to George Weissman, is based on creating specialized marketing niches and consciously shifting toward a lower-priced high-competition market. Management took pains to cultivate friendships with dealers, to build in extra-generous margins and to extend share ownership to key dealers. This dedication to strong distribution and market efforts is a persistent theme in Philip Morris' strategic planning.

Opportunity and expansion were fed by an imaginative advertising campaign. First, through radio's "Call for Philip Morris," the new brand achieved instant recognition. Strong advertising was supported by fundamental corporate policy: a high-quality product, strong product image, aggressive distribution tactics, premium dealer profit margin and memorable advertising.

During the next three years, company profits more than quintupled and the stock offered to tobacco dealers at $10 per share soared to $70 per share, says Weissman, "thanks to the attitudes and ways of doing things which continue to form our company style today." These principles have prevailed at Philip Morris since the '30s.

The Philip Morris strategy is revealed most clearly in the revamping and promotion of Marlboro. The development of a single product in a line of over 140 products and its continuing domination of the market is a classic example of Philip Morris' methods. Here all the principles of aggressive marketing, slogans, exploitation of radio and TV, and major advertising were applied, such as linking advertising to cultural trends; linking the product to popular, widely viewed TV shows like "Gunsmoke" and "Bonanza"; and identifying the product with John Wayne, a national folk hero. They have tinkered with and simplified the campaign, but Marlboro is still the number-one cigarette in the United States and number one internationally.

GROWTH AND RESPONSE TO CHANGE

The CEO holds the purse strings and has the first and highest order of responsibility for directing the investments of the corporation. This means allocating the capital resources to the core purpose of the business. He must have an objective, dispassionate attitude to the various business lines and traditional older products, as well as an openness to risk, changes in direction and novel areas of investment. Here the CEO faces competing demands from executives to invest in accordance with their particular interests.

Aware of the competitive advantages as well as the hazards of too great an attachment to the past, the CEO must respond to change by anticipating the future. In managing for future growth and balanced expansion, the CEO must have the fortitude to buy as well as sell. He must have the courage to divest and acquire companies and the strength to make a radical turn in direction—away from diminished or marginal businesses to new, expanding sectors of the economy. He needs to conceive of growth in relation to the corporate culture and the managerial talents in the corporation and avoid mergers or acquisitions which weaken rather than strengthen the corporate core.

The shaping of a growth strategy requires the CEO to make far-reaching, long-term decisions in divestitures, diversification and acquisition. Acquisitions, often viewed as a fast-track growth strategy, are of particular interest. Acquisition by the CEO of companies that are vertically integrated is a comparatively simple operation; acquisition of completely new, unrelated businesses—diversification by acquisition—is an infinitely more complex procedure.

The Sears diversification and growth strategy was achieved

by reorganizing the corporation and streamlining it almost as a precondition for acquisition. Its corporate investment strategy was a model of excellence: Telling dealt from strength, identifying a growth sector of the economy, and hitching Sears to that star. At the same time, growth was contained within the nationwide merchandising base of the company.

With over 800 stores, coast to coast, with high visibility and strong customer loyalty, Telling defined a set of goals based on past experience—meeting the merchandising and insurance needs of the American middle class. Adding the financial services of consumer banking, residential real estate and personal investments to the existing core was a brilliant form of diversification, completed without changing the corporate culture or losing touch with the company's unique purpose as a business entity.

The acquisitions program created an immediate base for rapid but controlled future growth by integrating the new companies into a strong corporate retailing operation that could nurture the growth.

Seeking to move from a single product in the late '50s, Philip Morris acquired the first paper-making and packaging companies. In 1972 the company took over the Mission Viejo Company, designer and builder of large-scale, planned communities in California and Colorado. It also acquired a group of companies that made chewing gum, razor blades and shaving cream, all linked by high turnover, low-unit cost and similar market outlets. Despite the natural fit with management interests and abilities, these companies required almost as much management, time and energy as the cigarette business did. Since, at the same time, they did not generate enough profits, they were sold.

These negative early experiences with diversification resulted in the search for opportunity and led to the purchase of Miller Brewing, engaging the company in three tasks:

- To make Miller a significantly larger factor in the beer industry
- To change the perception of Miller's principal product, High Life, from a beer for the country-club set to a product

for workers
- To develop a product portfolio for Miller—a family of brands for different market niches like the one Philip Morris already possessed in cigarettes

Robert Anderson of Rockwell is an ideal spokesman for diversification in American industry. Directing a $9 million sales, high-tech, multi-industry corporation, he defines the role of the CEO in managing four distinct businesses in a broad variety of markets, affected by different business and economic cycles. An advocate of diversification, Anderson describes how this complex balancing act is conducted.

In order to strengthen its diversified role, Rockwell redeployed its assets and pruned away a number of businesses which did not fit within the core. Between 1978 and '82, it divested businesses with total sales of over $1 billion. Thus, diversification was strengthened by divestiture. Anderson notes that unlimited diversification can be worse than no diversification at all. Here the balance of business between government and commercial markets, and among different segments within these markets, served to enhance diversity, spread the risk and maintain a steady course through the peaks and valleys of the market cycle.

It is revealing to read how Danforth and the corporate management committee of Westinghouse manage this giant business, functioning as 26 separate and largely autonomous business units, and operating with a high degree of independence. All growth resources—capital, strategic funds and R&D—are corporate property controlled at the top. He describes the linkage of finance, technology and marketing and defines how Westinghouse is subject to one broad strategy tied to quality, productivity, portfolio direction, growth and innovation, executive development and communications.

Change and response to change are the underlying themes of Danforth's view from the top. He reviews and examines the 100 years of Westinghouse experience in three major historical divisions and demonstrates how its leaders have reoriented the business to survive and grow. It is surprising to learn that Westinghouse is only one of ten companies in the

Fortune 100 list to survive over 100 years—a sure test of adaptability and executive leadership!

The corporate history of Westinghouse is marked by aggressive acts to exploit new inventions like the electronic light bulb and electrical energy. Time and again the company capitalized on technological advances which, in turn, led to new business, such as radios and electrical home appliances.

For those who remember Betty Furness and her television commercial of the '50s, "You Can Be Sure If It's Westinghouse," it is remarkable to realize that this giant corporation had abandoned the appliance business by the mid-1970s. This flexible and open approach to the future health and survival of the corporation—the painful need to cut out, divest or shut down a major business of long standing—is properly identified by Danforth as among the "toughest decisions" a CEO must make.

The critical insights revealed in Brown's account of the AT&T breakup clarify how he negotiated the corporate divestiture so as to respond to inexorable, external forces and yet position the new corporation to grow and succeed in an intensely competitive economy.

Brown describes the underlying economic, technological and legislative forces which created an irresistible need to change. The almost incredible fact that Ma Bell—the most successful and efficient monopoly in the world—had to break apart in order to survive was no longer a contradiction in terms, but a necessity for survival. The basic decision to negotiate and conciliate rather than resist made it possible to extricate AT&T from a quagmire of issues. "Trapped in the middle of a three-ring circus—with no ringmaster in sight," Brown felt that time was running out and the Congress, the FCC and the Justice Department would never reach a consensus. Thus, he made a most difficult, painful and fundamental decision—namely to accept fragmentation as the price of progress, to regain the initiative and to devise a new and different role to carry AT&T through the next century of high-tech progress.

Wendt conceives of the organization as an organic model. He strongly favors and supports a commitment as CEO to the fundamental core purpose of SmithKline Beckman, i.e., health care.

He relates the structure of the future corporation to his organic model. Wendt uses this model to reject diversification of the corporation by the acquisition of unrelated businesses.

Critical of the "rage to diversify" that swept American business in the '60s and '70s, Wendt hopes that this obsession has largely spent its force. He cites the diversification of SmithKline Beckman in the '60s as a fundamental error and goes on to describe the divestiture of industrial businesses in 1983 that returned the corporation to its organic purpose, namely the health-care business.

Wendt readily admits that industrial businesses did not fit into the SmithKline Beckman culture and that the company had insufficient management expertise in their administration. And he applauds the company's decision to move out of these areas and devote undivided attention to its substantial positions in the therapeutic, diagnostic and analytical fields of health care. This move, he believes, created a sharper definition of the corporate purpose and brought performance closer to his vision of the new model of the corporation.

MOTIVATION AND MANAGING PEOPLE

Motivation is a popular word. However, it is difficult to achieve, especially in large multinational corporations such as those discussed in this book. Managing a highly educated professional work force—and motivating them—in a complex enterprise requires the highest order of management.

The key concepts discussed by the contributing CEOs involve a series of philosophical and ethical considerations. They also indicate strong attachments to the new managerial concepts of teamwork, employee involvement in decision making, employment security, opportunity for personal growth and a fair system of rewards and penalties. Significantly, these CEOs are deeply concerned with the meaning of work, including the proper balance of work, family and leisure in contemporary American life-styles.

Wendt integrates motivation with his broad philosophy of the modern corporation; Danforth relates managing people to the future of Westinghouse; Oreffice considers personnel management as his first order of resonsibility; and Anderson suggests that decision making should be pushed down to the lowest practical level.

A critical principle, according to Wendt, is the development of a model of the corporation that motivates employees, and a management that emphasizes the importance of motivation—thereby improving the quality of working life and enhancing individual productivity.

Wendt suggests four major steps the corporation should take to motivate employees:

- The purpose or central objective of the business must be understood by all hands—that is, the corporation's core purpose should be central and clear
- The corporation should be organized in relatively small units so that people know each other personally and feel close to the leader of the unit
- People within the organization should have common bonds, both personal and organizational, which unite people as people, not simply as co-workers
- The personality and leadership of the CEO and other leaders should personify the corporate culture

Wendt also believes that there must be incentives that "encourage long-term employment, a feeling of job security and a sense of trust in the company's leadership."

Danforth takes us into the realm of the CEO's daily world and speaks frankly about his management style—the essence of delegation, trust, leadership and high tolerance for bad news. He points out that the management of a company's employees has become one of the most difficult problems in recent years because of the introduction of robots. In the long run, alternative jobs will be available, but in the short run, managers must deal with worker displacement. He speaks forcefully about the human resources of Westinghouse and the corporate commitment to employment security, describing how employee turnover can be managed under normal circumstances to limit layoffs. In addition to these attrition techniques, Westinghouse has other means of achieving employment stability, such as using a cadre of temporary employees during peak work periods to protect the core work force during slack times. Here is a CEO who has the vision and commitment to the future to believe in and defend the corporate goal of lifetime employment for employees throughout a huge corporation.

Oreffice takes pride in the fact that he is designated by people in the company as the "phantom personnel director." He takes this nickname seriously, and appropriately so, because he sees the role of the CEO in this large multinational corporation as ensuring that the right people are in the right job at the right time.

The people skills that seem important to Oreffice in a manager are the ability to detect poor performance in employees before it becomes a problem and to communicate with and motivate discouraged employees; the ability to delegate authority; and "the necessity to recognize that there's an appropriate time to step aside and make way for the next generation of managers in the organization."

Anderson suggests that forward-looking companies today are peeling away cumbersome layers of management and that "decision making authority is being pushed down to the lowest practical level on the hierarchical ladder." He notes other changes in the way companies deal with employees, such as quality circles, suggestion programs and other channels by means of which employees at all levels help to find better ways of doing things. He stresses the importance for employees to take responsibility for their own actions and reports that at Rockwell and other forward-looking companies, employees are encouraged to take charge of their own decision making through statistical process control. In this program, a machine operator is responsible for the quality of the parts being produced, a process, says Anderson, in which basic responsibility is restored "where it belongs—at the place and time of product creation."

At MCI, says McGowan, an effort is being made to avoid empire building, which results in the proliferation of layers of management and staff. "We're constantly working," he says, "to push decision-making responsibility *down* in the hierarchy and *out* in the field. We're flattening the management pyramid."

McGowan believes that electronics is helpful in reducing the layers of management, i.e., when a company is linked up, data can be entered anywhere in the organization as events occur—and managers can call up the necessary information by pressing a key. According to McGowan, there is then much less need for layers of middle managers "to aggregate and massage that information and pass it along the chain of command."

Direct access information, said McGowan, makes for more efficient management because as message takers and givers proliferate, information tends to become distorted. He is convinced that the more layers that are introduced, the less likely it is that anyone—least of all the CEO—will really know what is going on.

DECISION MAKING

The delicate balance between centralization and decentralization of power lies at the heart of the decison-making process. Delegation of the power to make important decisions is a function of the CEO's style of leadership—he will decide what kinds of decisions will be delegated and at what level of the organization decisions will be made.

In times of crisis, it is natural for the CEO to feel a heightened sense of responsibility and to be less willing to delegate authority to make decisions. In normal circumstances, the CEO is more likely to retain only the most serious decisions and to delegate others to the various levels of management. In tune with the times and the current interest in participation, decision making in many companies has been pushed to lower and lower levels of management and of the entire work force, and this has been remarked on by several of the CEOs.

In each of the chapters the CEO describes complex, far-reaching corporate decisions which affect the future of the business and the manner in which they were reached. In almost every case, the writer has also commented on the question of delegation of decision making as a key issue in corporate management.

In his role as counselor, Ford seeks to restrain the urge to make decisions and, instead, favors delegation to the people who have responsibility for execution of the decisions. Ford says that increasingly he tends to delegate day-to-day decisions to the people who have to implement them. In some instances, this may require that he, as chief executive, "may need to negotiate differences—and develop compatability among staff, line employees and shareholders." "It's a balancing act," he says, "orchestrating the skills of the various managers and people necessary to the operation of the company." His goals are similar to those of each of the CEOs who have contributed to this book.

In making decisions, Philip Morris has never followed the hierarchical command structure found so often in large corporations. The structure is essentially collegial and attempts to sustain a small-business atmosphere in corporate headquarters. Managers are encouraged to act as colleagues and fellow entrepreneurs. Top managers still visit the trade, attend marketing conventions and make retail calls. Individual offices are small and unintimidating; doors are mostly kept open; and there is heavy stress on keeping employees informed and involved. "Ideas are solicited and evaluated in terms of what they are, rather than where they come from," says Weissman. "If people of ability and spirit, at whatever level, are not encouraged to speak up and given all the responsibility they can handle, there's no point in hiring them."

Oreffice describes the need for an appropriate degree of delegation of authority to build confidence and experience down the line.

Dealing with the issue of crisis management, Oreffice counsels the manager against overreacting to the crisis and suggests that he or she keep a clear sense of proportion. At the same time he favors the strong interaction of key people within the organization, stressing the need for joint consultation and group assessment of the crisis situation.

At Dow, he divides crises into those that are implicit business opportunities and those that are severe threats to the survival of the business. He stresses the need for early-warning programs, and cautions as to the degree that managers must centralize authority or minimize and reduce the degree of delegation during crisis periods. Then he points to the need to relax the reins and redelegate as promptly as possible. In other words, he sees the issue of crisis management clearly as a CEO's responsibility and not one that can be distributed across the whole organization, since centralization is critical to speed, authority and firmness of results. Centralizing decision making during a critical period also fixes the responsibility for the crisis where the power rests within the organization.

ENCOURAGING ENTREPRENEURSHIP

In an era of accelerated change in education, technology and telecommunications, corporations of enormous size and complexity cannot allow themselves to become sluggish and oversized. Size itself can become an impediment, slowing movement and blocking change. Today, the fastest growing, most progressive companies seek entrepreneurship. That is, they seek to re-create a sense of community and an esprit de corps which encourage risk taking. Entrepreneurship within large corporations is difficult to achieve, however, unless organizational concepts of staffing, decision making and risk-taking are compatible.

The innovative organization is a rare species. It is ready to expose itself to change and radical ideas, it encourages and rewards risk-taking and it has the strength to tolerate failure.

To move on the leading edge, the organization needs to engage its highest talent and is increasingly attracted to the use of entrepreneurial teams—small, creative groups which often cut through the hierarchy to create a genuine spirit of smallness and speed.

Risk-taking, according to Wendt, is critical to corporations and their management, particularly when authority is delegated to literally hundreds of individuals. Wendt believes in giving people the freedom to take risks and the freedom to fail or succeed. He emphasizes that risk-taking goes hand in hand with giving more autonomy to smaller units within the corporation and allowing for greater experimentation, personal responsibility and motivation. He also stresses the necessity for sharing scientific findings across the products and businesses of the organization so that each element supports some or all of the other elements in the corporate model.

Wendt visualizes the need for structural integration in his model of the corporation of the future. He favors "smallness" over gargantuan size and sees the small company as more integrated, responsive and more sensitive. Thus he urges that large organizations be redesigned as collections of interlinking small groups to make teamwork possible. This concept is on the leading edge of developments in the most advanced corporations in the world today, where teams and small groups are innovating and developing a more competitive spirit.

Telling injected a new entrepreneurial spirit almost overnight at Sears by dropping the average age of Sears officers from nearly 60 to 48. Through a far-reaching early-retirement program, he created a leaner, more youthful organization, with new vitality. So complete a transformation is unheard of in a single generation of top management in a corporate giant the size of Sears.

Telling notes that success is important, but striving is even more important. He works to create a climate of intelligent risk-taking and a strong entrepreneurial spirit. In the final analysis, says Telling, "Everything starts with people." His experiences as a high-achieving CEO have led him to identify as the most important talents for a CEO the ability to pick good people, to put them in the right jobs and then to have the wisdom to stay out of their way. At the same time, he notes, "you want them to know that you are there when they need you."

An aggressive advertising campaign for a new product—Miller Lite beer—highlights the entrepreneurial spirit at Philip Morris, the parent company. With a third fewer calories than regular beer, Miller Lite was advertised with a positive thrust as "Everything you've always wanted in a beer. And less." This innovative new product was scorned by the industry, which predicted failure, says Weissman, but Miller had the competitive advantage and its ads forged a major success for Lite months before other brewers could begin to compete.

7 Up was the first caffeine-free, popular soft drink to compete with the colas. Philip Morris sought to model this acquisition on Miller's success by focusing on the national concern for physical fitness and weight control, but, in this case, competitive companies countered quickly with their own caffeine-free colas.

Philip Morris has retained an ability to seize new ideas and to develop them aggressively, in part because of the Philip Morris environment. Philip Morris hires "people of ability and spirit" and then gives them the opportunity to develop further and strengthen their entrepreneurial qualities. The audacious ideas and actions of these innovators have become a hallmark of the company.

Anderson underscores Rockwell's commitment to entrepreneurship. "We encourage entrepreneurship—making bold plans, backing them up and carrying them out. Sometimes that means making mistakes as well and learning from them. At Rockwell managers are encouraged to take the initiative to plan, invest and market their products and services as though they were on their own. And the company gives them as much latitude as possible in managing their own areas of the business.

Anderson sees the formation of small new companies—based on "one person's good idea"—and the creation of thousands of new jobs as one of the strengths of American business. As CEO of a giant corporation, he would like to see just such a "spirit of entrepreneurship" transferred to large and well-established companies. This approach, he believes, is important not only to individual businesses but to American business, in general, in terms of meeting foreign competition.

McGowan describes the entrepreneurial style of MCI in developing products with a concrete example. The company hired a small group of people who had demonstrated their creativity at other leading companies, he writes, and said to them, "You create your own organization and develop a new business. Develop it with our money, with our blessing and with our review." Nine months later, with the help of MCI's existing operations, this star-quality group had introduced a new business—MCI Mail—"on schedule and on budget." The product, which delivers messages either from computer to computer, or from computer to MCI's "electronic in-box" and then, on paper, to addressees without computers, within four hours, is the revolutionary new electronic equivalent of the postal service. Finding the best talent, supporting it with funds and services and then setting it free to create a new product paid off for MCI.

DEVELOPING EXECUTIVES FOR THE NEXT GENERATION

Among the many concerns of the CEO, the attention to executive succession is one of the most important. This most personal and sensitive issue affects the entire future of the enterprise. The selection of executives, their development, advancement and their separation are all decisions which concern the CEO.

In recent years, especially since the 1980-82 economic recession, a growing sensitivity to age has emerged. Executive burnout and seniority are seen as impediments to change, and stability is giving way to turnover, especially by means of earlier retirements. Youth and more open opportunity at the highest levels are becoming fashionable ideas.

Ford addresses the educational needs of tomorrow's executives in terms of a broad and highly varied educational background, favoring a leavening of engineering or liberal arts education with more attention to world history, international economics and politics. He points out that "since more and more corporations are multinational, the executive must also be multicultural."

Ford believes that the scope and breadth of education, in and of itself, will not sustain the executive over the long term. He notes that if executives lose their curiosity about the world, allow their intellectual interest to atrophy, restrict their reading to trade journals and periodicals and "retreat behind the balance sheets and the potted palms of their executive sanctuary," they will not fulfill the role of the executive in an effective manner.

The importance of executive development and selection is viewed by Oreffice as one of the critical and outstanding functions of the CEO. He describes the process of personnel selection, personnel development, the use of cross-functional developments and the application of a system of "deceleration" and phased early retirement as an active component of the executive development process. In addition, Oreffice stresses the necessity for a lean organization.

His chapter is devoted primarily to the deeply felt attitudes of a CEO on the development of executives who are committed to the goals of the organization.

The program of deceleration, which is unique to Dow, deserves special attention on the part of the reader. In this instance, Dow deliberately creates greater opportunities for younger managers by making room at the top. To deal with the need for opportunity at the highest levels and to compensate for burnout, the program of deceleration has been devised: a process of slowing down the activities of executives from being busy 110 percent of their time to a system of phased retirement. During the first year, the line management responsibility is removed and individuals may devote perhaps 80 percent of their time to the company, phasing down gradually in successive years by 10 percent decrements, until they ultimately retire from the company.

Oreffice believes that this deceleration program is valuable since it retains the expertise, wisdom and know-how of the senior management as independent managerial consultants. It also opens up the line responsibilities for the younger, up-and-coming future executives, who would otherwise be blocked or diverted from corporate careers. His description of executive selection at Dow indicated how the CEO and his management team, comprised of the presidents of six geographic areas and other key staff members, sort out and review the development and future for 1,000 key people in the organization. In the selection process Dow believes that the best interests of the employee's development are considered equally with the company's needs and in many cases, employee development is placed ahead of the interests of the company. Executive development cannot be measured in terms of day-to-day efficiency of performance. Rather, it is an investment in an individual who is expected to make a future, long-term, significant contribution to the enterprise as a whole.

In this respect, Oreffice notes that Dow does not believe in the process of executive development up narrow vertical ladders, but rather is committed to job enlargement, that is, the use of cross-functional training and development and movement of executives across major functions of the organization for which they have not necessarily had any prior training or experience. This functional cross-fertilization is seen as critical to tying the three key functions of Dow Chemical together, as well as integrating its six geographical areas.

CREATING A CORPORATE CULTURE

The concept of corporate culture, defined as the traditions, customs, and practices of an organization, is currently in vogue. Each organization has its own folkways and mores that have a persuasive influence upon employee behavior, but the CEO is the vital, living force who personifies the value system and embodies its ethics, moral values, business goals and esprit in his daily leadership style. Chief executives can sustain or merely maintain the corporate culture, but those who seek to consciously change it face an enormous challenge.

In this volume, many of the CEOs refer to the corporate culture as an element which integrates the many parts of the corporation into a cohesive whole, and they see their role as fostering this process.

Wendt believes that the CEO should articulate a corporate vision and sense of direction, motivate and cause others to motivate, reconcile conflict and personify the corporate culture and reward system. He sees the CEO as the nucleus organism of the corporation and as the regulator of its metabolism.

Wendt elaborates and clarifies the meaning of corporate culture as a social or anthropological aspect of the modern organization. Here Wendt points to a long series of corporate leaders who are informal, open, often idiosyncratic and educated in the classic liberal arts and sciences tradition. They impart to the corporation "the qualities of poise, integrity, common sense, purposefulness and good humor." These are the leadership traits which they treasure and visualize as significant. Wendt alludes to the amorphous and esthetic quality of the corporate culture and sees in it more qualitative rather than quantitative terms. This culture is an "ethical impulse" that radiates from the top down through the entire organization, and he admits that the ethical imperatives of the organization are always subject to the blemishes of misjudgment.

Philip Morris' vision is derived from a sense of being "outsiders or have-nots" with a corporate culture of having to battle harder and be different from the rest of the industry. This sense of being a "have-not" company created a culture that compensated for size by gaining ground through speed and outflanking its competitors rather than by engaging in head-on conflict.

Weissman refers to this underlying underdog spirit as a driving force which fuels the culture and encourages the leaders to remain competitively involved and forever striving. In this corporate culture, there is little room for the complacency or self-satisfied smugness that comes with giant size.

Philip Morris' corporate culture has an open-door philosophy and a strong competitive spirit. Weissman says that two reasons for success are resistance to complacency and depth and continuity of management. These two factors have contributed in turn to a successful corporate culture and a strong sense of corporate responsibility. A strong esprit de corps—a mixture of pride, competitiveness and team play—has also contributed.

After 14 years as CEO of Emhart, T. Mitchell Ford sees credibility as the sine qua non of successful, productive leadership. In this respect, he stresses the need for spunk and candor in presenting the corporation to its public: the financial community, employees, shareholders and the community at large. Ford defines his role as CEO as counselor, arbitrator and philosopher.

Rockwell International evolved from a series of mergers and acquisitions, from 1967 through 1974. Rapid growth, diversified industries, mixed managements and different corporate cultures all created the need to mold the corporation into a unified whole. Anderson states categorically that Rockwell is neither a conglomerate nor a holding company but, instead, an operating company with diversified manufacturing in high-tech businesses.

Indiscriminate mixtures of different cultures under one management often threaten the central core of a corporation. Anderson—and the other CEOs—are sensitive to this danger and keenly aware of the need for unity within diversity.

ESTABLISHING THE FOUNDATION FOR THE FUTURE OF BUSINESS

Reading tea leaves, or looking into a crystal ball may entice some futurists. It does not attract CEOs. Their view of the future of their enterprise is derived from a number of legitimate sources—and yet it is not fail-safe.

The future is not a well-traveled, familiar highway. It is unexplored territory, and charting it requires not only facts about the enterprise and about underlying economic, social and political forces but also certain intangible qualities on the part of the CEO: vision, insight, openness to change, to name only a few. Year-to-year or quarterly achievements are not harbingers of the future. Thus, members of the *Fortune* 100 today may not be among the corporate winners of the twenty-first century. Deregulation, world competition, inflation and the high cost of money have forced many companies into bankruptcy during the last decade, and the testing ground of the intermediate and long-term future may be even more severe.

Wendt considers the future in its historical context. He discusses the economic, political and social forces that have formulated the role of the modern corporation, drawing heavily on the foremost literature in the field. He documents his broad-ranging theoretical and philosophical analysis with references to some of the leading ideas on the role of corporations in our society. Wendt sees the large multinational corporation as in a state of evolution and traces the analogy to the military prototypes which are so common in the large corporations. Moving from his historical frame of reference, he firmly addresses the issue of what form the corporation should take in response to the demographic and societal changes in the twenty-first century.

Wendt responds to a major challenge in his chapter by seeking to rationalize and define the role of the corporation in the twenty-first century. In so doing, he discusses, in some depth, a set of guiding principles that he believes are critical to the purpose of the multinational corporation.

- The principal purpose of the multinational corporation is to pursue science and technology, to create value and then to introduce products and services which enhance the quality of life through human productivity
- The "demythologization of organizational assumptions." He describes some current myths and reduces them to reality, citing the negative effect of omnipotent managers in the organization
- The corporate model of the future must adapt its responses to both technology and humanization. The process of change in technology is incessant and requires a direct response on the part of all institutions, but most certainly on the part of the corporation itself
- The new model of the corporation must achieve a proper balance between the elements of consensus, review and the exercise of responsibility. He discusses consensus in the Japanese/American model and elucidates on the process of review as a process in corporate decision making

Brown now paints the future in exciting technological terms and we can sense the new energy and competitive forces which he has unleashed at AT&T. He wants it to enter its second century as a smaller, tougher, more energetic multinational corporation at the leading edge of telecommunications—a state-of-the-art giant stripped down for action, for progress and for success. Several goals capture our imagination:

- Establish a new standard of performance—a down-time objective of only two minutes per year
- Develop a million component microchip with a chip in tens of millions by the year 2000
- Transmit 420 million bits of information per second, error free, over 125 miles without amplification. This is equivalent to a 30-volume Encyclopaedia Brittanica transmitted in a few seconds
- Design remote controls for all types of appliances and heating and cooling systems
- Assign telephone numbers to individuals rather than telephones

Brown is excited about a future in which AT&T people will make major contributions to the telecommunications field. Marked by high standards, dedication, integrity, excellence and continuing achievement, how can this organization possibly fail? Brown has a great vision of the future—optimistic, strong and convincing—and he has already laid the foundation.

McGowan of MCI sees the future as a new and rapidly changing era that is being brought about by the emergence of new computer, telecommunications and information technologies. He sees these technologies as creating new opportunities in every industry; altering the structure of the markets themselves; changing production and distribution patterns; and changing organizations and the ways people work. And he believes that preparing for this information age and staying competitive in it is the single most significant management challenge of our time. "Companies and individuals who position themselves to take full advantage of the information technologies," he warns, "will gain the competitive edge. Those who do not, risk being left behind."

Anderson portrays the corporate future in terms that are evocative of the ideas of each of the contributors to this book. His summing up of American corporate trends is thoughtful, pragmatic and foresighted and serves, we believe, not only to depict his own view of the future but also to synthesize in a coherent whole many of the views of the eight other contributors to this book. He sees for the future:

- Diversification, as only one of the coming trends
- Streamlining of management structure, with leaner organizations peeling away cumbersome layers of management
- Decision-making authority pushed down to the lowest practical level
- Increased employee involvement in decision making, productivity and quality improvement
- Flexibility in the management organization, not limited to mid-level management reforms; an office of the chief

executive with three members to share executive and operating responsibilities; a corporate management committee that meets monthly to review performance
- Entrepreneurship—a major trend which will continue to change the American business world, engaging more people in making bold plans and making mistakes as well
- Internationalization of business, pointing to the need for industrial competitiveness without geographic boundaries
- Growing influence of computer technology on the future direction of business management. The problem is not how to use computers, says Anderson, but how to avoid misusing them

Overall, the pattern that emerges from these "views from the top" is of a thoughtful, innovative leadership, concerned with the future and willing to take the risks necessary to get there. Their collective effort leaves little doubt that "the top" is in good hands, and the foundation is firmly established.

Index